ANNOUNCING THE H
NOW IN PREPARATION F

The edition of *The Complete Works of Frances Ridley Havergal* has five parts:

Volume I *Behold Your King:*
The Complete Poetical Works of Frances Ridley Havergal

Volume II *Whose I Am and Whom I Serve:*
Prose Works of Frances Ridley Havergal

Volume III *Loving Messages for the Little Ones:*
Works for Children by Frances Ridley Havergal

Volume IV *Love for Love: Frances Ridley Havergal:*
Memorials, Letters and Biographical Works

Volume V *Songs of Truth and Love:*
Music by Frances Ridley Havergal and William Henry Havergal

David L. Chalkley, Editor   Dr. Glen T. Wegge, Music Editor

The Music of Frances Ridley Havergal by Glen T. Wegge, Ph.D.

This Companion Volume to the Havergal edition is a valuable presentation of F.R.H.'s extant scores. Except for a very few of her hymntunes published in hymnbooks, most or nearly all of F.R.H.'s scores have been very little—if any at all—seen, or even known of, for nearly a century. What a valuable body of music has been unknown for so long and is now made available to many. Dr. Wegge completed his Ph.D. in Music Theory at Indiana University at Bloomington, and his diligence and thoroughness in this volume are obvious. First an analysis of F.R.H.'s compositions is given, an essay that both addresses the most advanced musicians and also reaches those who are untrained in music; then all the extant scores that have been found are newly typeset, with complete texts for each score and extensive indices at the end of the book. This volume presents F.R.H.'s music in newly typeset scores diligently prepared by Dr. Wegge, and Volume V of the Havergal edition presents the scores in facsimile, the original 19th century scores. (The essay—a dissertation—analysing her scores is given the same both in this Companion Volume and in Volume V of the Havergal edition.)

Dr. Wegge is also preparing all of these scores for publication in performance folio editions.

The frontispiece in the original book, Never Say Die.

NEVER SAY "DIE."

A TALK WITH OLD FRIENDS.

BY

SAMUEL GILLESPIE PROUT

"Knowing her intense desire that Christ should be magnified, whether
by her life or in her death, may it be to His glory
that in these pages she, being dead,
'Yet speaketh ! ' "

Taken from the Edition of *The Complete Works of Frances Ridley Havergal.*

David L. Chalkley, Editor   Dr. Glen T. Wegge, Associate Editor

ISBN 978-1-937236-14-4   Library of Congress: 2011917963

Book cover by Sherry Goodwin and David Carter.

An illustration near the end of the original book, Never Say Die.

PREFACE.

This little book was not intended for publication. It was written, and a few hundred copies were printed, for distribution among some old friends of mine, in one of our great Northern cities. The present attempt to give the thing a wider circulation is mainly due to the indulgent judgment of one whose own works have long been fulfilling their recognized high mission, who believes that in its roughly-phrased thoughts are yet plainly set forward great Bible truths; and it is reproduced *without any pumicing.*

The earnest Christian friend who distributed copies of the book to those for whom, as an ungiven address, it was got up, wrote: "On Sunday about a dozen men were sitting on the flags in Charter street. I went up and told them that an old friend of theirs had sent them a book each. One of them read the title, and said, 'I never mean to say die.'" May those who shall glance at the cover of my little book but say *this* as their heart's resolve, with a lifted thought of prayer for the life that Christ is waiting to give to "every one," and it will matter little whether they look inside.

24th October, 1878.

PREFACE TO THE FOURTH EDITION.

In sending a Fourth Edition of my little book, I would gratefully acknowledge the indulgent reception of previous ones. There is, I am quite aware, in this unspoken talk with old friends, who could best appreciate very plain words, plenty of room for revision. Yet I have not attempted such—I do not care to touch the thing. To those who may object to its rugged form and homely utterances, I offer a few words of explanation. The first published edition of "Never say Die" was revised for press by the gifted and very dear friend to whose favourable opinion and most kind interest its publication is entirely due; and in a letter received from her at the time I am playfully commanded *not to alter another word.* She who wrote me that letter is now in "the land that is very far off"—at home in the palace of her King, for whom, through a life's loyal service, were used all her gifts of high thought and love-taught eloquence; and in the silence and shadow of "the hither side" her words of advice, which consent of hers cannot now qualify, have taken the sacredness of an injunction. Glancing, however, over the pages of my booklet, I note thankfully that there is in them *plenty of Bible*; and while in *that* fulness of "quietness and assurance" I can lose all anxiety in respect of faults of style and inelegancies of diction, I will hope that my readers may lose sight of them.

S. G. P.

Ilfracombe, December, 1879.

In his 1879 Preface, Samuel Gillespie Prout (1822–1911) was referring to Frances Ridley Havergal (1836–1879), who so much valued *Never Say Die*, edited the book for publication, and was a strong advocate for it to be widely read. Copied below this is an advertisement found in several 19th century books published by James Nisbet & Co., quoting F.R.H. on this book.

CONTENTS.

Another illustration in the original book, Never Say Die.

NEVER SAY "DIE."

I.

EASE her a bit—she'll do it yet,
If we can keep our foresail set.
That was a shave; well "Touch and go
Is a very good pilot," my lad you know.
Luff now—steady—the red on the white—
If that sea takes her, no harbour to-night.
Missed! No, we have it—how they cheer!
Why, half the town must be on the pier.
She'll want some patching, lad, by-and-by;
But I think we may call her the "Never say Die."

Never say "Die," in the wildest of weather.
Never say "Die," while the planks hold together.
And if she breaks up—a rent plank or an oar,
Though the craft make no harbour, shall float you to shore.

Over the long ridge—towards the sea—
That's where the first faint gleams will be.
I don't think they'll try it again to-night;
And our fellows are sure to be here with the light.
I *believe* there's a glimmer out there in the sky!
Hold on, and hold out, boys, and never say "Die!"
Never say "Die," when the night lingers longest,
Never say "Die," when the foe musters strongest.
As the last shot is fired, and the dull tramp is near,
In the grey of the dawn, come the clash and the cheer.

II.

Out on the black, drear waters—
    Where souls go darkly down,

And the terrible gleam of judgment light
    On the writhing sea is thrown!
Crouched in your foundering boat alone—
Mast, and rudder, and oars all gone!
In a brief dread lull of the tempest's might,
Drifting helplessly into the night—
Through the hurrying gloom, not one pale star;
Not one dim haven lamp out afar—
As you watch each inch of the water's rise,
Not daring to look on those awful skies;
Another light through the opening seam,
On your dull, unlifted sight shall beam.
Moan not out to the pitiless, drowning wave.
ONE is walking the waters—strong to save!

In the shattered fort, with clustering foes,
    Who neither tire nor sleep—
In the stern set fight through a life's dark night,
    And the weary watch you must keep—
Sore wounded, weaponless, all alone,
As the chill dark deepens before the dawn;
Alone with the fallen—stark and wan,
That dim, cold dawn shall look upon—
Dream not of yielding, nor flight, nor fear,
When " the blast of the terrible ones " sweeps near,
And through the rent wall, side by side,
The awful Leaders together ride—
Death and Satan, all their power
Shall pale, and pass with the morning hour:
In the dark, on that stained and cumbered ground,
The saving strength of the LORD stands round.

In the blackest surges that sin can roll
Over the wrestling, sinking soul—
Bent down on the brink of the fiery lake,
In the deadliest close of Hell's gathering might—
In the creeping gloom of Eternal night;—
Will you die—with Christ's hand outstretched to take?
With His love listening down, to catch your cry,
Never say to your soul, Brother—*Never* say " Die! "

NEVER SAY " DIE."

———

CHAPTER I.

NEVER SAY " DIE."

VERY likely some people will say I had better have put a text on the outside of my little book, than the three familiar words that are upon its cover. I don't know that I had. They are good hearty Englishman's words, full of pith and power. In the strength of them, many a poor little fort has been held by a handful of men against battalions; and many a poor fellow pulled to ground by poverty and misfortune—maybe by his own bitter fault—has shaken himself free, and has struggled up, a stronger man than ever for the tussle. It's true, they are not Bible *words*; but they hold, and in a somewhat "rough and ready" way they do plainly express, a strong, precious *Bible thought.*

Why, *it's all Bible.* Three times over, in those old days before Jesus Christ had come, God asks poor, self-destroyed sinners like you and me, "Why will ye die?" (Jeremiah 27:13; Ezekiel 18:31; 33:11.) Again and again, in other words, He repeats His question, *beseeching* us to "live"; and in the thirty-three years of toil and want and weary sorrow that the Son of God spent on His lost earth, but one complaint escaped the Saviour's lips—the heavy outsighing of His disappointed love—that the men He had come to save, *would die.* "Ye will not come to me, that ye might have life" (John 5:40).

Now, of course, dear friends, neither the Bible words, nor, in the sense I use them, the homely ones on the outside of this little book, refer to *dying,* in the every-day meaning of the word—to that most common, most solemn parting of the soul from the body, which is the certain lot of us all. "We must needs die"; "It is *appointed* unto men once to die"—says God to us. He asks, "What man liveth, and shall not see death?" More than that—His Word tells us concerning ourselves, "The living *know that they shall die*" (2 Samuel 14:14; Hebrews 9:27; Psalm 89:48; Ecclesiastes 9:5). The Bible must say what is true;

but of the greater number of us it might wonderingly be asked, *Do* they know? it doesn't look as though they did!

We honour and reward those who, at the risk of their own, "save life." What *is* saving life? Only putting off death. The one true Life Saver is the Life Giver. To all of us—in whatever earthly condition—in whatever spiritual state—must come sooner or later, the last drawn breath. Whether in a quick gasp of agony, or in quiet slumber, matters nothing—it will be *the last*—and *what then?*—"After this, the judgment" (Hebrews 9:27). *Now* we shall see what God means by asking us, "Why will ye die?" "The *soul* that sinneth, it shall die" (Ezekiel 18:4, 20). Something more here than the poor body that friends shed tears over, and the undertaker brings the coffin for, and the minister reads the service over—"The soul that sinneth, it shall die," not "may"—but a great, strong, Bible "shall."

I read again, "There is no man that sinneth not!"—"All have sinned." "The Scripture hath concluded all under sin." And all the while, God says, "Why will ye die?" Surely that is a strange thing to ask man, who is told at the same time that if he sins, he *shall* die. Ah! but God never mocks poor sinners: there must be some way out of this for us. We will learn it straight from the mouth of Jesus Christ Himself—"God so loved the world, that He gave his only begotten Son, that whosoever believeth in Him should not perish, but have everlasting life." "Verily, verily I say unto you, he that believeth on Me hath everlasting life." "Whosoever liveth and believeth in Me *shall never die*" (John 3:16; 6:47; 11:26). What *is* this *believing* that the Bible makes so much of—that *the never dying depends on?* "He that believeth on me"—"Whosoever believeth on Him"—what does it mean? How am *I* going to get hold of this believing; and the *never dying* along with it? Get hold of it we must, or there's no "everlasting life" for any one of us—"He that *believeth* on the Son *hath* everlasting life; and he that *believeth not* the Son *shall not see* life" (John 3:36). These are God's own plain words about the matter. These two lines hedge us in—there is no way over them, or out of them. Either we believe, and shall never die; or we don't believe, and shall never see life.

Some may say, "How you're dinning into me that Believe! believe! I *can't* 'believe' as you say." Well, change the word; call it "Come," and let us see what we can make of that. Now, if there are two medicines which have exactly the same effect in curing disease, it's no matter which of the two you take. One may be pink, and the other white—one may be sweet, and the other sour; but if they *both cure*, it is not of the least consequence, is it, which phial you empty? Let us set over against each other, two texts I have already given; both of them Christ's own spoken words—*both cure-alls.* "Ye will not *come* to Me, that ye might have *life.*" "He that *believeth* on Me hath everlasting *life.*" Again, in the same chapter of St. John's Gospel as the last text is taken from, there are six verses (35 to 40) in which the *coming* and the *believing* are so interwoven that you can hardly tell which is which. Men *die* of hunger, don't they? And so they do of thirst—"He that *cometh to Me* shall never hunger, and he that *believeth on Me* shall never thirst." The *never dying* for both. If we have come, we *have* believed, limping and fearing, very likely, at the best; but "Lord, I believe; help thou mine unbelief" (Mark 9:24), brought a man a wonderful mercy.

CHAPTER II.

BOUGHT WATER.

I DO want you, dear friends, to see this *coming* of ours very plainly. It's a thing each of us has to do for himself. No one can come for us, and come we must—get to Christ somehow we must—or say " Die " to our souls.

Here's a man lying wrecked upon a wild seashore; hopeless of aid—too weak and broken to scale the cliffs—perishing of thirst—driven half mad, as the ebb tide swirls in and out of rock-basins at his feet, by the gurgle in his ear of water that can never quench it. From the edge of the sea comes to him the voice of a poor forlorn shipmate, wrecked like himself. A feeble hail—heard as in a dream—"Hillo! there's a spring of fresh water out on these black rocks, close to low-water mark." Poor fellow, his mind's going! thinks the one a little higher up the beach; and he presses the parched lips closer, and lets the cruel sound of the washing water lull him to the death sleep. Yet again comes to his dull ear that faint hail: it seems further off than before—"Hillo! it's—quite—true." Staggering blindly towards the voice—he could hardly tell you how he got to his feet—stumbling at each step, falling over the jagged rocks, and into the deep pools—very hardly gained. Only a few score yards; but they seemed a day's journey! Yes—there it is—the bright, blessed water—bubbling up strong-ly from those briny depths. (I know just such a strange spring; one of God's hidden wonders.) And drinking—drinking—again and again, new life is given, and hope, and strength it may be, not only to drag up the steep, broken cliff-path his own bruised, wearied limbs, but to bear into safety the crippled ship-mate, who told of that precious fountain whose waters he could not bring.

Don't you see it, dear friends? A poor, lame sort of *coming* that—a *believing* that was most like doubt; and oh! how weak the brother's voice that hailed. But the blackening lips drank the water! There it was—there it *is*—"Living Wa-ter:" welling up—welling up—for you and for me; and we may dip it up with our soiled, trembling hands, and never thirst any more.

Yet one word about this water, of which God says, "Whosoever will, let him take the water of life *freely*." It is *Bought water*. In most of our cities, and often by the wayside, we find free public drinking fountains; and great boons they are, both to ourselves, and to our four-footed friends and fellow-workers. Some have been put up by humane, generous individuals, some at the City's charge, and opened with a good deal of ceremony; most of them bearing some inscription giving the date and circumstances of their erection—alike in this, that all were erected at no small cost, and all are *absolutely free* to every passer-by. The cool draught—be it a gallon or a pint—costs you and me nothing at all, and cost somebody a good deal. A clear gift to us, we get our need supplied, only because the full cost has been already paid. And just mark this—*only the thirsty ones* stop to drink.

Now, will you read with me a few verses of the 55th chapter of Isaiah? "Ho, every one that thirsteth, come ye to the waters, and he that hath no money, come ye, buy, and eat; yea, come, buy wine and milk, without money and without price." A strange sort of *buying,* that. Yes, very strange. God's ways are very strange ways, according to our ideas. He tells us Himself in this same chapter, a few verses on, "My thoughts are not your thoughts, neither are your ways my ways, saith the Lord." It was a very strange thing that He should give His Son to die—a very strange thing that Jesus Christ should be glad to leave heaven, and come to die—for such men and women as we know ourselves to be. "He that hath no money" *buys* all that his starving, thirsting soul needs—buys it of God, with His own treasure. *We* cannot pay God for anything that we want from Him, but we do not have His gifts for nothing: His own Son, our Saviour Jesus Christ, paid down the full price, or we, every one of us, through eternity, must vainly have craved one drop of water that might be borne upon a finger's tip.

"Ho, every one that thirsteth, come—whosoever will, let him take the water of life freely," are God's words, over His "Fountain—for sin and for uncleanness" (Zechariah 13:1). That was opened by Christ, free and brimming over, to quench a whole world's thirst, and wash away a whole world's sin,—when, upon the cross, He drank to its dregs for us "the cup of trembling." *Do you thirst,* my friends? I do not ask, Are you of those who "thirst after righteousness"? A great and sure blessing is *theirs* (Matthew 5:6). But are you simply *very thirsty?* Is your life parched and dry, and has all you have tried, to quench the miserable thirst, like wine in fever, only increased it? "Come ye to the waters." If we do not thirst, we shall never stop to drink. And if we do not drink, we die. Beyond the flow of that full, free, living stream, the thirst will come—in that terrible land where "no water is," and where "the light is as darkness."

I said just now that every one of us must come for himself. Quite certain that is—there are not two words about it. But we do not come *of* ourselves: we have power given us to come, as well as the thing given that we come for. "Faith," we are told, which is but another word for believing, "is the gift of God"; and we have seen that believing is just coming, so that too must be a gift. Indeed, we are not left to make this out for ourselves. Christ has Himself told us, "No man can come unto me, except it were *given to him* of my Father" (Ephesians 2:8; John 6:65). There is a text in this sixth chapter of St. John (verse 44) which puzzles a good many people, and puts into their minds the very fear and doubt it should do away with. It is this—"No man can come to Me, except the Father which hath sent Me draw him." They are Christ's own words. He had been *inviting all* to come, and had just said (verse 37)—"Him that cometh to Me, I will in no wise cast out." Some one who wants to be saved, and, it may be, feels really sure that if he *comes* to Christ he *will* be saved, reads these words, and says, "Ah! but God *must draw me.* Of course, if He were to draw me, I should come; but it's clear I *can't come* unless He does; the Bible says so." Put it just the other way, my friend. *Have you* come? You *know well enough* whether you have or not. If you have come, since "no man *can* come" except the Father draw him, why, God must have drawn *you,* and this text with that other one we spoke of, in the 65th verse, are your best assurance that all is right. Every one who comes to Christ, *is led up by God to Himself.*

Do I know whether I have come? Of course I do. I must come to any one of you, surely, before I can speak to you; anyhow, I must be coming, I must have got within earshot, or where would be the good of my speaking? Well, *you know* if you have ever said anything to God—if you have ever asked Christ to do anything for your soul: if you have, *you have come*; and you will soon know in your heart that you have indeed come, *by your having got something.* That poor shipwrecked fellow hardly knew how he reached the strange spring. The sharp rocks, and deep black pools, seemed all a part of his dream walk, but with the freshness of that blessed, cool draught of water, and in the first faint feeling of new life it gave, he woke to the knowledge that he had indeed come—and was saved.

CHAPTER III.

GOD'S TERMS.

MY DEAR SISTER, my dear brother, who may read this poor little book of mine, do take from me God's message. "Why will ye die?" Never—*never* say "Die" to your own souls while God's declared will is that "every one" "may have everlasting life."

Oh! it is the *stupidest* thing for a man to die eternally—to say with a whole Bible full of Life offered to him, "Don't talk to me about your Heaven, and your Water of Life, and your loving Christ—*I* go in for Hell, and Satan, and Eternal Death!" I know you are horrified at the very idea of your using *such words*, but it's what you *mean*, if you "will not come" to the Saviour, for the life you can get nowhere else. You must be saved on God's terms, or lost on Satan's: and they are equally simple.

We have seen how simple God's are—one word expresses them—"Come." Satan merely says, "Don't go."

It's true he tells us to go on committing all those sins we are so fond of—that they are part of our nature, and we can't help them; but these *might be brought to the Saviour,* and his terrible account with the soul torn up: so, his master-word is, "Whatever you do, don't go near Christ—*no need* at all."

God pleads, "Why will ye die?" The devil brings out his old rubbed-up lie—"Ye *shall not* surely die" (Genesis 3:4); but, later on, when he and death are coming close up, to look into your deathly white face, he whispers awfully, "*No good* at all, you *must* die."

Dear friends, do not let Satan lie away your souls, to mock you all through eternity, with the terribly true taunt—(the devil tells men awful truths, be sure, in his own land)—"You sold them to me miserably cheap." It is the old sad story, eternally told, of the poor drunkard heir, who let his title-deeds go for a bad bank-note, and died in jail for passing it. Christ begs you to come to Him—

He says He certainly will not cast you out—and, of course, if you are not cast out, you must be taken in, and *are safe*. Why *should* you take Satan's word before God's?

Once in a barn, among a lot of hop-pickers, I noticed a fine, powerfully built man, with a resolute face, that had some stories in it; evidently, at first glance, an old soldier. He had seen a deal of service, I found, had been wounded more than once, and had led a strange life altogether. If he had served the Queen as well and as faithfully as it was quite plain he had served the devil, he certainly should have been promoted from the ranks. I told him so, and earnestly pressed him to change the service, and join "Christ's Own." The man's reply, given in a deliberating way, with the emphasis of one almost persuaded, startled me. "Well, I suppose Jesus Christ's a deal bigger than the devil." A very great deal "bigger," thank God! He is "mighty to save." "*All power* is given unto Me in heaven and in earth," He has declared of Himself. He is "KING OF KINGS AND LORD OF LORDS—able to save to the uttermost all who come unto God by Him" (Isaiah 63:1; Matthew 28:18; Revelation 19:16; Hebrews 7:25).

Make "certain sure," my friends, that *you* have come to Him. Don't say you "will think about it." It's not far. "The Lord is *nigh* unto all that call upon Him—to all that call upon Him in truth." "I, a God at hand" is what He says of Himself (Psalm 145:18; Jeremiah 23:23). Christ has already *come* to *you*—He is *close by*—waiting for you.

With God, remember, coming is having, asking is getting. Only come and *say something to Him—pray*, that is. Prayer is just the calling out of a want. To God, who understands "my thought afar off," the very want in my heart may be a prayer; not, indeed, a mere half wish—but a *felt need*. If, in a careless off-hand way, I ask another for dainties that I do not much care whether I get or not, *that's* not praying. When the gnawing hunger forces from my lips the cry, "For God's sake, give me bread," *that*, or but the dumb, upturned, famished face, *is a prayer*. We have *all a starving* need of Christ, and the bitterness of our need will be the measure of our earnestness.

True, our very prayers are sinful: they come out of a heart that is "deceitful above all things, and desperately wicked," and from "unclean lips"; and the Bible asks, "Who can bring a clean thing out of an unclean?"—and answers—"Not one" (Jeremiah 17:9; Isaiah 6:5; Job 14:4). A dear young friend once wrote to me, "Please never again call my prayers 'innocent'; I think sometimes they will be *very little prayers* when they reach the throne above—there must be so much sin in them that wants washing away first." All our prayers *want washing*; but if they are the crying out of our hearts, however deceitful and wicked those hearts may be, they *will* be washed, and they *must be heard*—for Jesus Christ's sake.

There is a special promise of hearing for *the thirsty ones*—"When their tongue faileth for thirst, I the Lord will hear them" (Isaiah 41:17).

But we must ask God for the eternal life He is anxious to give, in the only way He will give it. One meets constantly with people who quite believe they are going to heaven, though they have not the slightest warrant for such a belief. Easy-going people, who get out of their soul-difficulty by saying, "You know God's very good"; and have no doubt that somehow it will all come right in the end. My dear friends, if the end finds them thus, it will come awfully wrong. Surely, if God is giving us so great a gift as the salvation He has bought for us at that vast price we have been speaking of, He has the right to give it as He will. Christ has plainly said, "I am *the Way,* the Truth, and the Life; no man cometh unto the Father but by Me"; and we are further told, "There is none other name under heaven, given among men, whereby we must be saved" (John 14:6; Acts 4:12). *Do* you think we have the least right to expect to be saved, if we ask God to save us by any other name, or in any way, but "*the way*"? A man miserably poor, and with no character to speak of, half starved and half clothed, is told by a kind, rich friend to *go for all he wants* to a shop where his needs can be supplied. He has neither pence nor credit; but, says his friend, "Make use of my name, and they'll give you anything you want." If he would not use his friend's name, but persisted in asking for food and clothing, and all that he so badly wanted, on his own account, or gave the name of some companion as penniless and disreputable as himself, you certainly would not pity the foolish fellow if he went to bed hungry, and slept cold that night.

Christ, too, is everything to us, or He is nothing. "As many as touched were made perfectly whole" (Matthew 14:36). They had not to go to the doctor and get him to carry on Christ's treatment; nor might they think to help on the case by some "splendid stuff" of their own making, that they had at home. "Perfectly whole," by the one touch.

"*No* power in ourselves to help ourselves." "When we were yet *without strength*—Christ died for the ungodly." With a crushed limb, under a tree or a mass of rock that has fallen upon him, lies one—just as helpless as his youngest child, though the strongest man in the quarry, or on all the forest side—his feats of strength the talk of the country round. There he lies—can't stir an inch— that free, muscular arm of his cannot raise a ton! There he *must* lie, until a gang of his mates, with ropes and levers, come to him; happy that his shout has been heard. Now, just imagine that man pushing away at the crushing mass, all the while the levers and pulleys were at work, till the skin was all off his foolish palm; and saying when lifted up, broken and powerless—"Well, you've *helped nicely* to get me out!" Most of us, I'm pretty sure, have, from time to time, made a try to free ourselves from the weight of sin on our souls; and have fallen back bruised and tired out—we shall never *so* get from under—*only one Arm* has "put on strength" for the task; and we poor struggling sinners, as rebellious, as weak, are bidden to "take hold" of that strength (Isaiah 27:5).

CHAPTER IV.

BLUNDERS

THERE are people who tell us Christ was given for our example; and that we have only to follow it, to get to heaven. Does *God* tell us that? He tells us indeed that Christ *left us* an example. Here is the passage—"Christ also *suffered for us,* leaving us an *example* that ye should follow His steps" (1 Peter. 2:21). Of the people in heaven, we are told that they are "found" of Christ, "without spot and blameless." How about "the garment spotted by the flesh"? We are told further that they "have washed their robes and made them white in the blood of the Lamb. *Therefore* are they before the throne of God" (2 Peter 3:14; Jude 23; Revelation 7:15). If you can so follow Christ, that you are just like Himself—"without blemish and without spot" (1 Peter 1:19), very certainly, you may walk unchallenged into the golden city—but whoever you are, *you'll want the password*—"JESUS."

Look you, my friends, when anybody talks to you about being saved by Christ's example, ask him how it would fare with a man who could not swim a stroke, struggling in deep water, if another, for all the aid he gave, kept swimming round him, calling to him, "Look! strike out like this," instead of clutching hold of his hair. The man would be drowned, that's all. Down he would go to the bottom, with his last despairing gaze fixed upon the strong swimmer, whose "example" could not save. Taking Christ's *example only* as our hope of salvation, is simply saying "Die" to our souls.

Now, very possibly, some Christian friends will say to you, "Oh! but you must repent first. Have you repented? You know we are told in the Bible, "Repent—and be converted." "Except ye repent, ye shall all likewise perish" (Acts 3:19; Luke 13:3). Repent? of course you must; but it may be—God grant it—that you *have* repented!

What *is* repentance? It is *not* penitence. That is a very different thing, and one that we must earnestly ask God by His Holy Spirit to give to each of us, as He has promised to do (Ezekiel 36:26, 27; Luke 11:13). *Penitence* is conviction of sin and sorrow for it. My question to you is again—Have you *really come?* If you have, then I believe that, in the Bible meaning of the word, you have *repented.* Repentance is a *change of mind.* That is the meaning of the word in the language in which the New Testament was originally written. A man is walking sturdily upon the wrong road—in the very opposite direction to that he should be going—every step taking him further from the place where he wants to find himself. Perhaps it is a black, starless night; and as he tramps on into the darkness, suddenly, across a bend of the road, he sees the far off glimmer of the city lights where his home is; and, on the instant, comes the thought, "Why, what a fool I am! I'm going the wrong way." And the man stops sharp, and then and there he turns round—not merely changes the step, but "Right about face"—and begins to retrace his weary walk. When that man stopped to turn right round, he *repented*—he changed his mind altogether about the way he had to go.

When you and I, my friends, pause in our blind, resolute tramp along the road "that leadeth to destruction" (Matthew 7:13), and ask ourselves with a sudden, startled cry, Why! where *are* we going?" we *repent.* When the poor prodigal, in that tender story Christ told of the Father's love, said, "I will arise and go to my father," he certainly repented. The story says, "He came to himself"—"and he arose and came to his father" (Luke 15:11–32).

The turning round, indeed, which is the *first step of the coming,* is not so easy for us. We must have a hand on ours. "Repent, and be converted" might perhaps be cast into the words, "Stop, and let God turn you." We are indeed *bidden* in the Bible to turn, but the turning no less than the believing is "of God"; and we read these prayers: "*Turn Thou me,* and I shall be turned"; "Turn Thou us *unto Thee*"; "Turn us, O God of our salvation" (Jeremiah 31:18; Lamentations 5:21; Psalm 85:4). "*All things* are of God." He "giveth" them: the turning—yes, and the repentance. *That* is one of Christ's especial gifts. He is "exalted—a Prince and a Saviour, for to give repentance—and forgiveness of sins" (Acts 5:31).

How often we hear such words as these, "Poor fellow! he's gone, died early this morning. At last. Well, his sufferings were dreadful—a happy release!" *Was it?* If he had repented, if he had *come to Christ*—yes. And if he had not come? Tell me, would you call it "a happy release" to take a man racked with pain from his bed, and fling him into a foul, dark dungeon?

There is another very terrible blunder some make as to God's dealings with us. They think because in this life they have had a tremendous share of its bad things—beggary and sickness, tormenting pain, and wanted sympathy—that they will, *on that account,* get the good things of the next life; that somehow it will be all made up to them by-and-by. Surely that's a very foolish sort of a hope. Fancy a man pleading before the magistrate, who had committed him for a robbery with violence, that he'd had a miserable life of it ever since he could remember—never had been so unfortunate a fellow. Would the warrant be suspended on such a plea? If it were, I think the man himself, however glad to get off, would not speak very reverently of the magistrate.

All the best things of heaven are ready, and waiting for *every one of us.* That rich man, whose parched tongue still craves one drop of cooling water, might have had them just the same as Lazarus (Luke 16:19–31); but there is no balancing of joy and sorrow, no making things square in the next world. From earth's brightest home we may pass into outer darkness, from its lowest depths of misery to "joy unspeakable and full of glory"; or the gladness of this life may unfold and brighten into that eternal joy and gladness, the woe of this life deepen into eternal gloom.

There is only one way to secure the for-ever joy, only one way to miss it. It is sure to "him that cometh," for ever missed by him that "will not come."

I recollect hearing a few words of a conversation between two men—squalid, washed-out looking fellows, both of them, with hardly manhood enough to keep them on their feet, and, it was sadly evident, no better acquainted with "Godliness" than they were with that virtue's proverbial next-door neighbour on the lower floor. One of them clearly felt himself to be a grievously undervalued, sat-upon individual, and bemoaned greatly the unmerited ill-success of so virtuous a life; yet hopefully ending his pathetic complaint with the words, "Ah, well! it will be all right when I gets to glory"; upon which comforting assurance his seedy companion simply remarked, "A rum sort of glory!" Strangely awful words. One could not dare to smile as the thought came, "These two men have got to live for ever!"

Have you thought of what is folded in these two little words—*for ever?* Any of you who have been to a funeral have heard read the solemn words, "This mortal must put on immortality" (1 Corinthians 15:53). *Your* mortal—*my* mortal. There is no getting away from it. Whatever we may wish, whatever we may dread, *we have got to live for ever;* and living for ever out of Christ means an ever-dying—means *a soul in the wrong eternity.* The Bible, which tells us truth about everything, tells us that Satan's home, where he receives his children, "prepared" for himself and his angels—never for us—is as eternal as the house with "many mansions," where Christ welcomes "His own," who have come to Him.

We speak of men whose lives and deaths were alike terrible, of whom we have read in history; or, it may be, people we ourselves well know; and we say of such, who died in the full mad rush, or in the settled stupor, of their sin, " Wasn't it awful?" Yes, indeed, awful!

And they are living now—have been living ever since—will go on living as long as God Himself lives; and, *in one eternity or the other, we* shall go on living too. Do think of these things, dear friends. They are tremendously real.

We do not, the most of us, feel them so. We feel this close-home-to-us life, in which we eat and drink, laugh and groan, work and want, real enough; but the reality of the world to come, somehow, we cannot get hold of. You doubt not for a moment the realness of the familiar street you go up and down, nor of the house in it where you live, of the food and clothing and shelter you need, and the hardly earned money that pays for them. All these things are quite real to your senses—substantial, everyday facts—often very uncomfortable ones. And so they *are* real, with reference to your bodies; but then the body is not *the man*. It is the least part of him, though "fearfully and wonderfully made" as it is (Psalm 139:14), it certainly claims better treatment than it gets from very many of us. That mysterious, never-dying soul of yours, that you may set little store by, and that "Christ poured out *His* soul unto death" to save (Isaiah 53:12), is your very real self; and, of course, the real things belong to the real man. The golden streets of "the city of the great King," the "white robes" and "harps" and "crowns of gold," the "treasure that faileth not," the "rest" that "remaineth";—the "mist of darkness—reserved for ever," the "dimness of anguish,"—"where their worm dieth not, and the fire is not quenched—there shall be wailing and gnashing of teeth"—these things, of which if any one speak it seems such strange, dreamy talk—these dreamy things are *the realities*; because they are *the for-ever things*; while all the rest—be it "joy" or be it "affliction"—"is but for a moment." An unspeakably precious "moment"—for in this awful little life of ours gather the eternal realities; yet, in view of these, " but a moment" (Psalm 48:2; Revelation 4, 5, 7; Luke 12:23; Hebrews 4:9; 2 Peter 2:17; Isaiah 8:22; Mark 9:44; Matthew 4:9; Job 20:5; 2 Corinthians 4:17).

Could you now be assured that years of happy life were yours, as happy as a man could possibly spend—*all but one second,* which certainly would be agony unspeakable—the thought of that one terrible moment would hardly trouble you much. You would say, "Why, however bad it may be, it will be gone before I know anything about it." Or say, you were as surely doomed to a life of utter, hopeless wretchedness—*all but one second* of the most exquisite joy: would you get from the promise of that one second's bliss, that would be past before you could realise that it had come to you, any comfort in the long dreary years of sorrow and weary pain? And yet, we could take pencil and paper, and by a simple sum, you or I could soon set down the number of seconds in the longest life; but no arithmetic will show how many millions of the longest lives ever lived on earth, multiplied again by the number of all the rays of light that ever left the sun, go to make up that one life which must begin for every one of us, when we leave this world. Dear friends, mine are very poor words; but I am speaking to you of *real things*; and you and I, in "the first five minutes of Heaven, or the first five of Hell," shall *know* that they are such—shall find out the wretched nothingness of the shams we have all along been thinking realities—and that we have *begun living "for ever."*

I wish you would stop reading now; lay down the little book for a time, and try to think this thing out; and to help your thought, take with you that solemn question Christ asked so many centuries ago, and that no one has yet answered—"What is a man profited, if he shall gain the whole world and lose his own soul?" (Matthew 16:26).

There are so many ways in which a man can say "Die" to his soul. He may shout it out to that poor soul of his from the hoarse, scorched throat of the drunkard, in the fierce defiant oath of the blasphemer, in the reckless song and awful laugh of the profligate. Or the terrible word may be hissed from cold, unloving lips, that are seldom parted to talk of anything but their hoarded money or their selfish schemes; or whispered to the poor silly souls in quiet, comfortable homes, from which the light of God's Word and of His love is snugly curtained out. The word is the same—"Die, Soul—die!"

With some one voice or other we, every one of us, have said it to our souls, over and over again; and but that God's ever-waiting, never-wearying love stayed the mad bidding, I should not now be writing, you would never read these words.

No need of violence to kill either a body or a soul. A man dies just as surely by the laudanum dose that stupefies him into eternity, as by the swift bullet through his brain, or the plunge from the bridge parapet. And you may brick yourself up in forms and ceremonies and religiousnesses (which, mind, are not *religion*), and so suffocate your soul; or you may lull it to death by the pleasant poison of a fancied good life, just as effectually (if in God's mercy you are not shaken out of your deadly sleep) as by the life of daring, open, determined sin in which a man terribly says to the Saviour who "shall see of the travail of His soul and shall be satisfied" (Isaiah 53:11), "He shall get no satisfaction *out of me.*" Sheer soul-suicide—all of it alike.

CHAPTER V.

RAGS AND RIGHTEOUSNESS.

WHEN you do come to Christ, remember you can bring Him nothing but your sins. Your heart? Well, that's the very core of the ulcer, "deceitful above all things, and desperately wicked" (Jeremiah 17:9). You *can* bring nothing but sins; a bitter gift, but it is all you have to offer Him. Just you bring them! God knows what to do with them—He will take them from you, and will cast them behind His back (Isaiah 38:17). *That* is what God does with our sins that we bring to Him—He does not keep them to look at.

But bring them *at once*—do not you keep what God wants to put away. Besides, sins fester so. One of old found that out bitterly when he "kept silence." Very remarkable is that psalm (the thirty-second) from which those two words are taken. David was troubled fearfully about his sin, and we read, "I said, I will confess my transgressions unto the Lord; and Thou forgavest the iniquity of my sin." He had been thinking—thinking about his sin, till, as we should say, he was "worn to a skeleton." "My bones waxed old—my moisture is turned into the drought of summer." At last he says, "I *cannot* bear this sin of mine any longer. I really must tell God of it. I *will* confess it." "*And Thou forgavest!*" How God must have been *wanting to forgive* that sin—listening for the faintest thought in that poor torn heart towards Himself! Surely there is something *for us* there.

And another reason for bringing our sins *at once* is, that if you keep a sin by you, it is sure to take to itself "seven other." Sins are so dreadfully fond of each other's company. Yes. Bring each and every sin in its own day to Him, "who forgiveth all thine iniquities" (Psalm 103:3). Some old hateful sin it may be, that has been brought so often, your very soul turns sick as you lay the foul thing again at His feet. Tell God, if you will, you have done for yourself now, it is all over with hope. His word to you will be, "Thou *hast* destroyed thyself, but in Me is thy help" (Hosea 13:9).

Some one may object here—Well, but since we are told that "the Lord knoweth the thoughts of man"—that "all things are naked and opened unto the eyes of Him with whom we have to do" (Psalm 94:11; Hebrews 4:13), what can be the good of our bringing to God sins He knows all about? A father may know perfectly well that his child has been disobedient, but his *knowledge* of the offence would be no claim to its forgiveness; the child, surely, must come and ask for that.

Only do not think to *bring* Him any miserable bits of good—your respectability, or your morality, your regular church-going, or "charity," or any other of the poor stuff we think so much of. The Bible has one of its strong expressions for such. The Bible does use very strong language, but, you see, it deals with very strong things—strong sins, strong temptations, strong Satan, and, as we have thankfully seen, *an all-strong* Saviour. "All our righteousnesses," it tells us, "are as filthy rags" (Isaiah 64:6). Nice, decent clothing, that, to go before a king! God can do nothing with these good doings of ours. The blood of His Son will not wash them: their mock whiteness cannot take the light of Jesus Christ's righteousness, any more than it can bear the light of His judgment-seat. You may be, in many respects, in advance of your neighbours: you may be sober and kindly and honest, and lead a quiet, decent life,—altogether a thoroughly respectable person, and having the goodwill of all your friends, and of the neighbourhood. So much the better for your health and comfort—so much the better, very likely, for your purse—so much the better for the neighbours: but if *that is all you have* more than others, not a whit the better for your soul; you have only the "filthy rags" to stand up in.

Jesus Christ has told us, "Except your righteousness shall exceed the righteousness of the scribes and Pharisees, ye shall in no wise enter into the kingdom of heaven" (Matthew 5:20). Many of these Pharisees were, of course, the "hypocrites" that our Lord in another place calls them; but some of them, we may not doubt, were sincere, conscientious men, as "righteous" as men can be of themselves; but because it *was* their own righteousness, it would not do for heaven. One of their number could write of himself—and quite truly, for he was writing by the Spirit of God—that he was, "as touching the righteousness which is in the law, blameless." I wonder which of us could say that of himself. Anyhow, this "righteousness," if we had it, would be no more good to us than it was to St. Paul, who goes on to tell us in very plain words what value he himself put upon it. What he wanted, and what you and I want, is "the righteousness which is by faith of Jesus Christ unto all and upon all them that believe"—in other words, which is given to every one that comes and asks for it. The robes of the King's Son are put upon the ragged beggar, that he may go into the King's palace—nothing else goes in (Philippians 3:6; Romans 3:22, 23).

This is what the Bible calls "justification." Let us make it out quite plainly, for it is everything to us. It is what we "come" for, and through which alone we get the *never dying*. It is just our being looked upon by God, and treated by Him, as though we had never done one wrong thing, or thought one wrong thought; and thus, as being fit to "enter into the Kingdom of Heaven."

Justification, it has often been said, is paying in full our debt to God's justice. Yes—but it is *more than that*. A kind-hearted friend of mine, a county magistrate in North Wales, had a man brought before him for vagrancy, or some other petty offence, and had no option but to inflict a fine, with some days' imprisonment in default. The poor fellow had not a copper about him, so his committal was made out. As he was about to be removed, my friend signalled the constable to come over to him, and, while saying a few words, slipped into his hand the amount of the fine. Of course, there was no further talk of locking up—the small penalty was paid, and the man was free. This was certainly *paying a debt to justice*; but the magistrate did not take that vagrant home with him to his comfortable mansion, and make him one of his own family. Moreover, no offence had been committed against himself—the man owed him nothing; the sum, too, kindly given to pay the fine was a mere nothing out of the giver's wealth. The case stands very differently between us and God. Our whole debt is owed to the justice of Him who "emptied Himself" to pay it—"once" and "for all." It's the *bought water* over again; God is Creditor and Security in one. And it's not merely a debt—it's a crime. A miserable traitor, I must surrender my forfeited life; and am told that the *Prince has suffered in my stead*—that the law cannot punish in me the crime another has paid the penalty of, and that the King wants me with Him in His own home!

Christ in my place—that's "justification."

Very plain and strong the Bible gives us this most marvellous truth. "He hath *made Him to be sin* for us, who knew no sin; that *we* might be *made the righteousness of God* in Him" (2 Corinthians 5:21). "*Made*" righteousness—*we* have nothing but *unrighteousness*. We must, you see, get utterly rid of that wretched thing *self;* must cut it adrift—fling it overboard—have done with it altogether.

One now for ever free from the burthen[1] put this into strong, homely words that I like to remember. When first he fell fatally ill, he, like so many of us, thought his simple, honest, "good" life would do to go on into the other world;

---

[1] "Burthen" is an old form of "burden."

but God's Spirit showed him *it would not do at all,* and what alone would—*that righteousness* we have been talking about. Speaking to me one day of his new standing-ground, and his old terrible mistake, he said, "Yes—I see it all now, plain enough: *I must go slap over the wall."* He was a gardener, his garden and mine adjoining each other; and when he was coming to work for me, instead of coming round to the front of the house, he would put up his step ladder, and drop over the wall separating our gardens. No doubt this was the idea in my kindly old neighbour's mind at the time; getting at once, without any roundabout walking, out of his own garden, where he worked, and watched his vegetables grow with so much satisfaction, into another, in which he possessed nothing, and where his only right to be was that he was *told to come.*

Dear friends, let us all go "over the wall"—clean out of our own poor gardens—we can take none of their produce in our hands. If you *will* bring your good living and your precious righteousness to Christ, *you must make sin of the whole lot*—there's nothing else you can do with it—and ask to have it all forgiven: the man who *will* be saved by his own righteousness, says hopelessly "Die" to his soul. You must cast all this splendid rubbish of yours *on the heap*—along with the oaths and the lies, the drunkenness and Sabbath-breaking, and the foul living—and let the ever-flowing stream that keeps eddying round wash it all away.

There is no big sin—no little sin: sin is sin. "The thought of foolishness is sin," says the Bible (Proverbs 24:9). One such thought, though we may regard it as but a grain of sin, *must be* washed away—a whole mountain *may be* washed away—"into the depths of the sea."

That's a very wonderful idea we get in the text these words are a part of: "He will subdue our iniquities; and Thou wilt cast all their sins into the depths of the sea" (Micah 7:19). We are told that the extreme depth of the Indian Ocean is equal to the height of the loftiest mountain on our globe; and so, God's sea of mercy covers and conceals the highest mountain of sin that we can pile up towards heaven. Perhaps—I don't know—the loftiest snow-peak of the Himalayas might peer above the highest lifted wave of the Indian Ocean; but in God's ocean, mountain on mountain of sin, cast into its depths by His own hand, sink, lost, and ever hidden from the sight of God Himself. Priceless or worthless, anything dropped into earth's deepest seas could never be brought up—never be seen by us again. No fathom-line can sound their depths. And God's sea of love cannot be fathomed by His line of judgment. That sin, committed in long past years, the remembrance of which, though it has been confessed, and, for Christ's sake, forgiven (1 John 1:9), is often very cruel to us—that sin was cast by God, when we brought it to Him, "into the depths of the sea"—*God knows nothing about it.*

And—"He will subdue our iniquities." What a mercy *that* is! The mountain of sin has been brought, and has been cast into the depths of the sea, and forthwith—we begin to pile up another. We want our iniquities subdued, as well as our sins covered. One mercy were little good to us without the other—Jesus Christ, who was "made sin *for* us," "is—made *unto* us wisdom, and righteousness, and sanctification, and redemption" (1 Corinthians 1:30), and when we come to Him, we must ask for *all He wants to give us.* I know there are people who say, if a man comes in faith to Christ, he is saved—and there's the end of it. He *is* saved, but there is *not,* I think, the end of it. True—God's Word thrice assures us (Joel 2:32; Acts 2:21; Romans 10:13)—"Whosoever shall call on the name of the Lord shall be saved." Undoubtedly, the man who has called *from his heart,* were that call his last breath, is saved—from God's repeated assurance, it must be so; but if that man goes on living, if he would not go on sinning, he must keep on coming to the "fountain opened for sin and for uncleanness." As an old and deeply taught Christian minister once said to me, "It's *an ever first coming* to Christ." That's a wonderfully touching story that is told of a Staffordshire collier, a man who had for years been a leader in blasphemy and cruelty, and almost every conceivable sin, but who, by the power of Christ's constraining love, had become "a new creature" (2 Corinthians 5:17), and had given up his whole large heart to the Saviour:—how, when he was pressing upon his old companions that saving love he had himself found so precious, and one of them mockingly called out, "Eh, Ben, lad, it's loike thou'll soon be a-swearin' again wi' th' best of us,"—the full-souled, just saved Christian, unable to bear the thought that he should ever again blaspheme the Name now so dear to him, knelt down at the pit's mouth, and prayed that, sooner than he should utter another oath to grieve his Saviour, God would let him die where he knelt: and his prayer was granted. While his scoffing mates stared at that kneeling man, he had entered "through the gate into the city." *We* may not be *taken* from sin, but we must earnestly pray to be *kept* from sin. If we ask for a saved soul, we must also ask for a pure life—that is *God's* idea of salvation (Jeremiah 33:8; Ezekiel 36:25–27; Matthew 1:21; Ephesians 4:20–24; 1 John 1:9). God hates sin in the very same degree that He loves sinners. He *so* hates it as He "*so* loved the world," that He gave His Son "to put away sin" (John 3:16; Hebrews 9:26). Shall we have the face to come to God, and ask Him for the salvation "His unspeakable gift" brought us—and tell Him we mean to keep the sin too?

What would you think of a man who, ragged and filthy, had been brought to a hospital with the worst form of a terrible fever; who, by unresting care and the best skill, had been brought safely through; and weak, but well, washed and newly clothed, passed out of the gates to go and seek stealthily for the old, foul, fever-soaked clothes that were stripped from him when he entered? You would think the man was simply mad. I think a good many of us do just that mad thing. The gate of God's hospital is always open—every case admitted. The Great Physician, who loves to receive the worst, whom He alone can heal, is ever waiting for them. And He does heal the most desperate cases—"from the sole of the foot even unto the head—no soundness" (Isaiah 1:6). And He gives us His own clothing to wear. And out from His presence we go, and hunt up an old sin; and, hugging the foul, pestilential thing to our hearts, we walk straight back into the old road.

I said the gates of God's hospital are always open. They are so, and the light from its windows ever streaming into the dark night, to draw into its many wards all sick and wounded souls. Yes, thank God! and *old* patients, familiar with its pure, clean rest, and loving care, and patient skill, full of the old terrible disease that has become their very life, may be taken in—"him that cometh," though once and again he may have entered those doors and passed from them, Christ, the Good Physician, will "in no wise cast out." But, dear friends, the solemn thought for us is this. The rotting limb may not have power to bear us one step nearer to those welcoming lights. In the creeping stupor of starvation and disease, the glazing eye may not be able even to look towards them. The soul-sickness may close in soul-death—outside the gates!

And the home! We do not read that the poor prodigal whose story we have glanced at, who had "wasted his substance," but who "arose and came to his father"—who had been kissed, and clothed, and feasted, and rejoiced over—ever went back to the swineherd's rags and the husks. Ah! how many of us have tramped sullenly back into "that land" where they are for ever having "a mighty famine." Have we not? Where are we now? At home, or turning to the old familiar road down the hill—or back in the "far country," wasting there the Father's latest gifts of forgiving love?

How many of us, my friends, must say, "*I'm not at home*—I know *that*"?

I come back to you with that straight question from God, "Why will ye die?" If you have never come to Christ—come now. If you have gone away from Him—come back.

CHAPTER VI.

TAKING SIDES.

SOME of you, perhaps, will say, "I daresay it's all right enough, but I don't take much account of this *religion*—I know all about it." Do you? Do you know *anything* about it? We will not trouble ourselves about the exact meaning of the word. We understand by "religion" something that many people have, and very many more have not—which has mainly to do with their souls, but even as regards their bodies, makes itself very plainly seen, keeping people out of drink and out of debt, in decent clothes and tidy rooms, making good husbands and wives, mothers and fathers, children and neighbours, truthful, and kind to all God's dumb creatures—for as good John Bunyan said, "A man's cat will show that he has a Christian master." A cruel man, of course, cannot *possibly* be a Christian. No doubt, people may be all this without being truly religious; but we shall hardly make a mistake in saying that those who are the opposite of any of it certainly *are not* religious.

And here may come in a word to not a few, who, because they see some of their neighbours who profess religion doing particularly irreligious things, jump at once to the conclusion that the whole thing is a humbug. "Look at your religious people!" Yes, look at them. They'll bear looking at with all your eyes, though not, perhaps, with a microscope. What *you're* looking at are only the make-believes. There could be no shams in the world, if there were no realities. Nobody would coin bad money, or forge cheques, if the real ones did not *get value*; and you would never refuse a good sovereign from the bank, because there were bad ones about in the market.

To go back a bit. Suppose you heard a man say, "Oh, I don't take much account of health"; you would not value your own health the less for so stupid a saying. "I make *no account* of money" even would not be a particularly wise rule of life. Pay-days *will* come. One reflection I would here very earnestly press upon you. Take a religious man, or what is a much better word, a Christian—a poor lost sinner, that is, who has truly come to Christ—and one who has not come, and will not come. Say, the Christian has been making a mistake in the whole thing—has been giving himself a world of worry and anxiety about nothing—that all he has talked about and that I have been writing about is a "pack of stuff." When both come to die, anyhow, they're on equal terms. You'll say, "Your Christian's short life might have been a merrier one." Perhaps, but not a happier; and now that the two men are going behind the veil together, if there's nothing gained, there's nothing lost. Each has enjoyed himself for a moment, in his own way: and now—it's all over with them both. But *if* the Christian is right—if there is an Eternity—if sin and judgment, and pardon, if Christ and Satan, Heaven and Hell, *are realities,*—where is the other? I will not attempt any illustration here. Put your plain common sense to it, my brother.

Well, now—what is your idea of this "religion"? Is it something that draws a man's mouth down, and turns his eyes up—that lengthens his face, and shortens his pleasure—that, in fact, doesn't leave a laugh in him, and makes him go about, always carrying a pocket full of tracts, and a heart full of dismals? I'm pretty sure that's the idea many have of religion. I don't know about the tracts—there's no great objection to having a few of them about one, at any time; but as for all the rest—as for the doleful dumps—certainly the brightest, bravest, happiest fellows I have ever known have been the religious ones. It stands to reason that it should be so—that the man who knows *whatever comes is right,* and *whenever* it comes *he's ready,* ought to be happy, if any one should. Surely the right idea of religion is something to live by, and work by, and die by. As the Bible puts it in that grand working text we find in 1 Timothy 4:8—"Godliness is profitable unto all things, having promise of the life that now is, and of that which is to come." A religion without that promise is beggarly to live by—a chill, shuddering thing to die by. "The real thing in religion,"—as some one said to a not over-friendly questioner, who was curious about his "religion"—"is what would enable either of us, if told he was to be stuck up in that courtyard at sunrise to-morrow, opposite a file of soldiers, to say, 'All right.' No other religion is worth the fillip of a finger."

We *all* want a religion that can be brought out, and made use of at any moment—an "all right" religion. Travelling once by the Plymouth express from London, I recollect a roughish-looking, coarsely-clad young fellow getting into a railway carriage where I was seated. At some small station, just before we got to Exeter, came the ticket collector, and there was the usual handing up, and punching, and repocketing of tickets. The young fellow only said, "Pass." The collector just gave a glance at him—"All right." He was one of the company's servants—he was known—*anyhow,* it would have been "all right," for he had in his pocket the carefully folded paper, creased and worn by frequent use—that made him free of the line. In the same carriage, a lady passenger, in the little flurry of the sudden demand, could not find her ticket; neither from glove, muff, purse, nor pocket, was it forthcoming: this being an express train, the collector was perhaps a little impatient, and that made the search more hopeless. The passenger must leave the carriage, and go on by the following train. There was no help for it—the company's rules admitted no exception—no interference, no expostulation availed. Well dressed—most respectable—but no ticket to show! And by that "next train" she might be too late for home. My friends, is it "all right" with you? Are you sure you have your tickets? "Well to be on the safe side," we often hear said. On which side are you?

Let us not forget that *taking sides* here means *taking service.* The question may be put into this form, Who is your master? Every one of us has made his choice—either for the easy service of God, who gives us eternal life when we enter it, or the hard labour of Sin, in partnership with Satan, whose wages of "Death" are paid when our time's up. One or other it must be—there's no half-and-half service; no half-and-half anything, indeed, will be found in God's Word. It's Christ or Satan—Life or Death—a hard and fast line between. "No man can serve two masters," says the Bible (Joshua 24:14; Matthew 6:24).

A good few of us think we can. He who tries to do so has the very poorest chance of ever getting into *God's* service. The *"wages"* will only be from the one terrible master; and he pays for the half time that he knows was in reality *all his*—a *full wage.* Satan is a hard master, but he defrauds none of their wages; they are paid up to the last hour.

Those of us who have served him *would rather not be paid*—would make Satan welcome to the life's past service, for the miserable instalment of the eternal payment received. Not so. His strict, stern word to each of his servants on that awful pay-day will be, "Take that is thine"—and we must take it.

The devil does not put all his servants to the same work, though he pays them all the same wages. Some he employs short time—their earnings have no deduction. The work may be spread over a life, or crowded into a year of terribly earnest service. An inch depth of water over an acre of land represents about a hundred tons. Collect it all into a reservoir, and you have not a pound more or less.

And, in the service of the Father's home, all God's servants are His sons and daughters—*the "gift" is one*—since it never can be earned, it must be so:—you may have gone up to the vineyard in the first hour of the morning—I, as the evening shadows were falling—eternal life for both of us.

"Choose you this day whom ye will serve" (Joshua 24:15). Let us just put together a very few of God's *shalls* upon this solemn question of taking sides. "I have set before thee—life and good, and death and evil," are His own words (Deuteronomy 30:15).

"He that being often reproved hardeneth his neck, shall suddenly be destroyed, and that without remedy—They that are far from thee shall perish—While they be folden together as thorns, and while they are drunken as drunkards, they shall be devoured as stubble fully dry—Then shall they call upon me, but I will not answer—they shall be driven to darkness.

"Whoso hearkeneth unto me shall dwell safely, and shall be quiet from fear of evil—He shall call upon me, and I will answer—My sheep hear my voice, and I know them, and they follow me: and I give unto them eternal life; and they shall never perish—My people shall be satisfied with my goodness, saith the Lord—The Lord God giveth them light, and they shall reign for ever and ever" (Psalm 73:27, 91:15; Proverbs 1:28–33, 29:1; Isaiah 8:22; Jeremiah 31:14; Nahum 1:10; John 10:27, 28; Revelation 22:5).

To be "on the safe side" is simply to be *on the saved side*—to have "received" Jesus Christ in our hearts, as our *very own Saviour,* and *in doing so,* to have "become the sons of God" (John 1:12).

CHAPTER VII.

A WONDERFUL GIFT.

WE have just spoken of " the gift of God," of which " this is the record, that God hath given to us eternal life, and this life is in His Son." Here is the record of another most wonderful gift, which " every one that asketh receiveth," that God " hath also given unto us His Holy Spirit." All God's servants, we said, are His children—" born of the Spirit "; Jesus Christ Himself tells us, " Ye must be born again," and immediately after, He says we are born *of the Spirit.* It is through God's Spirit that we become His children and can do Him service, and receive the gift of eternal life (1 John 3:11, 12; Luke 11:10; 1 Thessalonians 4:8; John 3:7, 8).

Dear friends, do not fear to ask for the Holy Spirit. There is no petition to which there is a surer promise of answer—" If ye then, being evil, know how to give good gifts unto your children: how much more shall your heavenly Father give the Holy Spirit to them that ask him?" (Luke 11:13). And yet many of us, I believe, though we have " come," are afraid, we could scarcely tell why, to offer that prayer: there seems to us something so mysteriously awful in asking God for His Holy Spirit.

The text we have just read makes a very simple matter of it—as, indeed, the Bible does of everything that we poor sinners *must have.* Depend upon it, the Almighty has not wrought one link too many in His wonderful chain of strong love that lifts our dead, heavy souls to heaven. Surely, to think that we can do without any gift He freely offers is far greater presumption than to claim it.

We want God's Spirit to sanctify, no less than God's Son to redeem us. Christ, truly, " is made unto us—sanctification and redemption ": He is " all in all "; yet He has Himself taught us, in the words that promised to His sorrowing disciples the Holy Spirit for their all-sufficient " Comforter," that through the Spirit, who guides " into all truth," we learn " all things." We " have access " by Him "to the Father," to tell all our wants and troubles. And when, conscience-stricken and sorely perplexed, "we know not what we should pray for," "the Spirit itself maketh intercession for us." Through His might we are made alive—made free—made strong (John 14–16; Ephesians 2:18; Romans 8:26; 1 Peter 3:18; 2 Corinthians 3:17).

I think we all know something of the power of *another spirit*—"the spirit that now worketh in the children of disobedience,"—that often works terribly *in our hearts,* where, too, is always billeted that wretched old enemy Self:—God's Spirit, "the Spirit of life in Christ Jesus," will fight down all our strong foes, within and around, if we will but call for His aid. Well might one of old pray out of the gloom of his sin, "Take not Thy Holy Spirit from me" (Psalm 51:11).

Dear friends, we must let God give us *All Himself:* nothing short of that stupendous gift will meet the need of one sinful, struggling human soul. I was told of a poor half-witted Irish boy, who had got fast hold of this marvellous truth, and with his dying breath—the so long vacant face lit up with wondering gladness—exclaimed,

> "I see—what do I see?
> Three in One, and One in Three,
> *And all for me!*"

"O God! give me the grace of Thy Holy Spirit, for Jesus Christ's sake." These were the last words written in his Bible by a young man, my neighbour at the time; not, indeed, strong in intellect, but strong in simple faith, and who is now "for ever with the Lord." Why should not we all make them our earnest prayer?—we have seen from God's Word, that it is sure to be granted. The atoning blood of Christ upon our souls—His living Spirit in our hearts—to have this, is to have that complete Saviour who is the *one utter need* of every one of us;—all empty talk this,—if it does not bring my fellow-sinners and their Saviour together.

CHAPTER VIII.

SAVIOUR AND JUDGE.

In the war of a few years since, between France and Germany, a young French officer, starting hurriedly in the early morning, upon outpost duty, was offered a copy in his own language of "A Saviour for You," a little book well known, probably, to many of us. Giving a quick glance at the title, and thrusting the book into the breast of his tunic, he said, "A Saviour! Ah! that's what a man *wants* when the bits of shell are whizzing here and there—what we especially need, now that we are for ever in the field of battle."

I like to read of that dear boy who had but a few weeks left his mother's home, when the ship he had joined went into action. Through a long and heavy engagement so active and happy was he in every duty permitted him, that his bright, fearless face attracted the notice of the captain, who, at its close, summoned him to the quarter-deck, and expressed surprise at his cool bravery—so young, and in his first fight. "Please, sir," replied the noble little fellow, "I had a word with God in the crown of my cap before it began."

That's a fine story, too, that is told of the God-fearing captain of a coasting-vessel, whose calm happy look, when she had struck upon a rock and was settling fast, utterly amazed his crew, who thought he had lost his senses. "Why, captain," faltered one of them in utter terror, "one would think we were making our harbour. Don't you know we shall all be at the bottom in five minutes?" "Less time than that, lads," answered the captain with his quiet smile, "but I shall only drop into the hollow of my Father's hand." Man and boy, both "on the safe side"—"Ready."

Possibly none of these risks may be ours, but leaving even out of the question *all* the hazards and accidents of life, we want a Saviour—a received, accepted Saviour—none the less.

How many sudden deaths do we hear or read of almost daily! Think of that wonderful heart of yours, beating its hundred thousand strokes without stop or stay, within the twenty-four hours, forcing through tiny vessels, smaller many of them than the finest hair, twenty-four hogsheads of blood—of the nearly twenty-six thousand times you draw breath in the same number of hours, and of all the little valves and delicate hinges that are for ever opening and shutting and turning in that strange factory, your body, where the busy contractor Death keeps his workmen always on the premises. A very little hitch in the machinery, and the neighbours say to each other in their morning chat—of you, or of me, it may be—"You heard how suddenly that poor fellow in the next street went off?"—the unfinished work lying on the bench—the unopened book or the half-written letter still upon the study table—the hastily flung down rake under the lilacs, in the pleasant garden. The man has been before his God, and is gone into eternity.

The doctor says, "Can't live over two hours," and your ear catches the words. What would you care to be told that a princely fortune had come to you, not a pleasure earth could give that it would not ensure? Would you not put up your hands to shut out the very bearer of the news? "What's the good of talking to me about fortunes? Why, man, didn't you hear what the doctor said; don't you know I shall be gone in two hours?" Can any one assure us we shall not be gone in two minutes?

While I have written these few pages at least two hundred thousand souls have entered the eternal state. And now, as I stop a few seconds for a thought, another twenty, maybe thirty, souls *know* what heaven or what hell is. Why should not yours or mine have been of the number? "Well to be on the safe side." Yes, such a fatal, such an appalling thing to make a blunder here.

If you were starting on a journey from one of our large city railway stations, where there are many fast-following departures from the same platform, you would not say, "Oh, any train will do." You would make quite sure that you got into the right one. Yet say you *took* a wrong train, you might get the right one at some junction; or even from the distant terminus might return, and end your journey at home. If you embark for the wrong port, you may, at the worst, work your passage back. Forty or fifty years of your life may have been one long failure. Opportunities of making your way in the world may have been given you again and again, and again and again been lost; and you say, "What a fool I've been! I shall never have another chance!" Yes, you may. Some years of happy, healthful, useful life may yet be yours. "Never say die" has a brother proverb always in company—"While there's life there's hope." The *might have beens* are bitter, and often terrible; yet a hope may steal into them—"while there's life";

but oh! dear friends, the black utter despair of the lost idiot soul, that has to say all through its eternity, "I might have been in heaven."

Prison walls may be high, and the barred doors strong, and the moat wide and deep, and the sentinels armed and watchful; but patient daring may elude or defy the guards, and scale the walls, and swim the moat; and the dreary prison days may become but a strange dream, in the safe quiet of home. But when once the key of the eternal prison-house is turned on those who would not have their soul's debt paid for them, "they shall never see light." And Christ, who so wants to save us, holds that key; and His hand it is that turns that key! "He shutteth up a man, and there can be no opening" (Psalm 49:19; Isaiah 22:22; Revelation 1:18; Job 12:14). My dear fellow-sinners, might one bring to the unsaved *Dead*—to those who for the last fatal time have said "Die" to their souls—God's own four words that are in the first page of this little book, a hymn of awful joy would ring up to the very Throne that would still the angels' songs! Across the "great gulf fixed" comes no pleading call—we cannot do the dying twice over. "It is appointed unto men once to die, but after this the judgment."

I quoted that text, you will remember, at the beginning of our talk; we will take with it another—in effect the same, yet which may help our thoughts upon this most solemn certainty: "We must all appear before the judgment-seat of Christ" (2 Corinthians 5:10). There the words are—and they begin with a "must"; we cannot get away from them. It's a thing we *have got to do,* like the living for ever.

Let us read the text through:—"We must all appear before the judgment-seat of Christ: that every one may receive the things done in his body, according to that he hath done, whether it be good or bad." That's an awful look-out for you and me!

Stay! it is "the judgment-seat of *Christ*"—of the same Jesus Christ who said, "He that believeth on Me hath everlasting life—him that cometh unto Me I will in no wise cast out." "I came not," He says, "to judge the world, but to save the world" (John 12:47). To each of us poor condemned sinners—self-condemned and God-condemned, "tied and bound with the chain of our sins,"—Christ says, "I will come to you—may I? I knew that *I must come to judge,* and that is why *I came to save* (John 5:22; Luke 19:10). Yes, I am to be your Judge—*but not now*—let us talk this thing over." "Come *now* and *let us reason together,* saith the Lord: though your sins be as scarlet, they shall be as white as snow: though they be red like crimson, they shall be as wool" (Isaiah 1:18).

Shall we imagine (I believe I have met with this thought somewhere) a man in prison, waiting to be tried for his life—knowing that the evidence is dead against him, that the verdict must be "Guilty," that the sentence must be—Death. He is assured that though if he leaves his cell, to see his judge's face for the first time, nothing can save him; yet the judge is at heart his friend. True, he must be taken into the assize court, and must hear the verdict; but if there, in that cell, he will but let the judge talk with him—will make a full confession to his ear alone, there shall be no rising to give sentence—no dread black cap; he shall stand in the awful hush of that crowded court, to hear the terrible, *true* word "Guilty" from the foreman's lips, without pallor or trembling—a full free pardon, with the king's broad seal upon it, in his breast, to produce before them all—good in every court in the realm. What would you think of that man if, not knowing at what moment the gaoler[1] would enter his cell to take him into court, he refused contemptuously to see the judge who so wished to be his friend—shouted to him through the bars to begone, or said he would think about it—the visit might put him out in his meals, or spoil his sleep.

What would you say of him? "What an awful fool the man must be!"

Truly—an awful fool! And how about you and me, and this prison-life of ours, with its coarse pleasures and its heavy sleep, that may at any moment have a terrible awaking—and the ghastly gaoler[1] who will come to summon us—and the "great white Throne" out there—and Christ, the loving, patient Judge, at whose presence heaven and earth shall flee away, waiting, waiting here? "Behold, I stand at the door and knock," are His own wonderful words (Revelation 20:11 ; 3:20).

> "Death comes down with noiseless footstep
>   To the hall and hut;
> Think you Death will tarry waiting
>   For your door is shut?
> Jesus waiteth—waiteth—waiteth—
>   But the door is fast.
> Grieved, away the Saviour goeth.
>   Death breaks in at last!"

[1] gaoler: jailer

CHAPTER IX.

MARVELLOUS LOVE.

DEAR friends of mine, we must have the love before the judgment.

The love! *That* seems all that one poor sinner really wants to speak about to other sinners. I spoke a little while ago of a Bible full of life; it's all love, from one end to the other. Some one may say, "There's a deal in it too about a wrath and judgment." There is—in God's Word we need to shirk nothing. We find there terrible declarations and appalling pictures of God's "righteous judgment," and of "the wrath to come." He "will not at all *acquit*—and who can abide in the fierceness of His anger?" And it is just here, in this awful gloom of judgment and wrath, which *no sin can escape*—that the love comes out so wondrous bright and strong.

No sin can escape. The *sinner* can, if he will—because the stern judgment was passed, and the fierce wrath lay hard upon Christ, "who did no sin—made sin for us," "who died, the just for the unjust, to bring us to God—which delivered us from the wrath to come"; and so, we are "redeemed with judgment," and—"hereby perceive we the Love" (Nahum 1:3–6; 1 Peter 2:22; 3:18; 1 Thessalonians 1:10; Isaiah 1:27; 1 John 3:16).

Nothing but love would be of the least use to any of us; God's love is our life; we cannot get away from it. It is like the air we breathe, out of it we should die; that's not quite it—if we had not been *ever in it*, we should be dead—twice dead.

"Why will ye die?" comes the message from God to us all; and to all He sends marvellous words, that fill His own pleading question with such deep wonder. To each of you, my friends, whatever you have been, whatever you are, I will dare to say whatever, even now, you are meaning to be—to each *this* astonishing message is sent, "Yea, I have loved thee with an everlasting love" (Jeremiah 31:3).

And many a one will say, "How *can* God love me? Do you know what I am?"

No, I do not, but *God does*—and He loves you, and He *has been loving you all along.*

You cannot think too badly of yourself. The same Bible that tells you God loves you, tells you what *sort of a claim you have* to His love. "The Lord looked down from heaven upon the children of men, to see if there were any that did understand, and seek God. They are all gone aside, they are altogether become filthy: there is none that doeth good, no, not one." "Abominable and filthy is man, which drinketh iniquity like water" (Psalm 14:2, 3; Job 15:16). Well, there's not much *to love* in that description of what God sees in us all—nothing to make Him want us home with Him up in His pure heaven—is there? No wonder that you or I should say, "God love *me!* I *might* understand His having mercy on me; but that He should *love* me—*that's* too good to be true." No, it's quite true; and as though the Almighty, who so strangely loves us, would say, "I do not wonder at your trembling doubt—it must seem impossible to you, this love of Mine," He *underlines,* if I may so say, His own surprising message, and to assure our hearts, calls thus to each of us poor "filthy" sinners, "YEA, I *have* loved *thee.*"

Dear friends, is our poor human love weighed and measured by deserving? Tell the mother, whose heart is hungry for news of her reckless, unloving son, who has done his worst to break it, how utterly unworthy he is of one tender thought, and her reply will be, "Yes—I know; I love him—my poor boy." That's the answer—and the end of it. A mother's love is a very strong—a very precious thing. You, my dear young friends, who yet have loving mothers, do prize them as God's very best gift to you, in this life of weary work, and of many a sorrow and care. I have always felt that the love of a mother helps us to our nearest conception of how God loves us, yet—says His Word, "They *may* forget." God *cannot:* His is "an everlasting love."

And God loves us *just because He does love us.* I do not understand it; I don't believe the great angels round the throne understand it,—less, it may be, than I can, for they do not *need* the *love* as you and I do; but I am *sure of the love itself,* I am sure of this, that had God for one poor minute left off loving me, I should not now be talking to my fellow-sinners. Sin and Satan are awfully strong, but they are not strong enough to push back the love of God. "God *is* Love" (1 John 4:8, 16), and so there must be love enough to pardon every sinner's every sin. We cannot use up God!

An all-seeking love, an all-forgiving love—this "love of God" is also an all-knowing love. *That's* a mercy: you may think it anything but that, *but it is.* As

a poor woman said in her sin-sadness, "I can tell God I am sorry when I *can't
tell people.*"

Some friend whom I had deeply injured might assure me of his tender love,
and, in an agony of self-reproach, I might reply, "No, you cannot—you *may*
not love me, you *must* know it: I have wronged you in every way I could." And
the terrible telling of those wrongs might deservedly, and for ever, lose me that
friend's affection. Should I expect him with a quiet smile to say, "Oh yes, you
beggared me—you blackened my name—you robbed *my* life of love—I have
known it all along"—and again assure me of his deep unchanged love? And
Jesus Christ does this. He to whom a poor sinner had denied Him truly said,
"Lord, *thou knowest all things*" (John 21:17), who has seen every thought in
each one of our hearts—we may hear *Him* say, replying to the fearful whisper
of our trembling lips, "Oh that sin; Lord, that awful sin—I cannot, dare not
tell Thee of it,"—"Ah my child, I know it well. I know all its weight, and all its
blackness: I had it with Me on the cross."

Dear friends, let nothing, *nothing* keep you from coming to Christ—from
coming to "Everlasting Love," for "Everlasting Life." Your life may have been
such as even your poor fellow-sinner could not listen to the story of. Your sin,
my brother, may fill the very blackest page in that awful book where our iniquities and our secret sins are so terribly set down (Psalm 90:8). It may be too hid-
eous for your own frightened thought to bear in the silence of the night, when
you are alone with its fearful memory. No, *not alone*—Satan is telling you in his
loudest tone, it never can be forgiven. *It can:* Christ's strong, quiet words (Mark
3:28), "All sins shall be forgiven unto the sons of men, and blasphemies wherewith soever they blaspheme," out-talk all the devil-shout.

That awful cruel sin—God knows all about it; and only waits for you to tell
it, to *forget it utterly.* That foul, festering wound of your soul is not too foul for
the Saviour's healing touch.

No soul is lost for its sin; but because it would not bring its sin to Christ.

Remember, all your sin, and all mine, *has to come* into His presence, either
to be forgiven, or to be judged. We must either bring our sins to Him now, or
take them before Him on the Judgment Day! Creep up—stagger up—get anyhow up to Christ.

I dare not say that the depth of our sin is the gauge of His love, but I do believe that those who want Him most utterly, *He wants* most pitifully. We read
a wonderful prayer in one of the Psalms—"For thy name's sake, O Lord, pardon mine iniquity; *for it is great*" (Psalm 25:11). And the man who prayed that
prayer *had* his iniquity pardoned. The battling soul that then cried to God out of
the depths had just the same claim that you and I have to lay hold on that Name;

and just the same wondrous promise as was given to him shall be our answer—"I will set him on high, *because he hath known* My name" (Psalm 91:14).

Oh! I know the almost impossibility of dragging ourselves up to God; how we feel fearfully that we are really loving the horrid thing that is eating away our souls, even while we are asking God to deliver us. We must *take it all,* dear friends—the sin and the love of it. Like that poor naked outcast in the tombs of Gadara, who, with the broken fetters and chains clanking on his bleeding limbs, must come to Christ with all his devils in him (Mark 5); just so must *we* come—the vile thought in our hearts giving the lie to the miserable prayer on our lips. Say, if you can say nothing better, "God, Satan tells me I am an awful hypocrite, and Satan tells me truth"—and *coming so,* let but the cry, which is but half a prayer, go from your shuddering heart, that your tongue is dumb to speak—"O God!—For Christ's sake———." He Himself will make a prayer of that poor broken thought, and will answer it in the fulness of His own yearning, listening love. His hand will sweep clean out of His judgment-book the page that is black with your sin.

That hand never wrote it there; our sins register themselves; *God only blots them out*—and the Book of Life is ever before Him. To lost, hopeless, *speechless* sinners God has said surprising words—"Before they call I will answer"; and *this* will be His answer to your heart's mute, miserable cry, "I have blotted out as a thick cloud thy transgressions, and as a cloud thy sins: Return unto Me; for I have redeemed thee" (Isaiah 44:22).

Does any one still say, "That all reads well enough, but there's no hope for *me,*—I know that; *I* am too far gone—hell-bound—my very soul is blackening and putrefying with the sin-poison." I can well understand such terrible words. They are not *too* terrible for many a soul's experience. My brother, let us *never* say "Die." Jesus ever liveth, and He ever loveth. Satan may be saying in malignant triumph, "By this time he stinketh." Christ will say, "Come forth."

In every word that Jesus Christ said there must be very deep meaning. Such a depth of all-saving love is in those most precious words that He spoke to the ruler who came to Him by night—"As Moses lifted up the serpent in the wilderness, even so must the Son of Man be lifted up; that whosoever believeth in Him should not perish, but have eternal life" (John 3:14, 15). It may be that when the Saviour spoke those words to Nicodemus, He thought of *you* who now are saying to your soul, "No hope."

"Even so!" We must turn to the event to which those words of our Lord refer; the old, sad, wilderness story of Israel's sin, and of its bitter punishment, with yet the light of a strange mercy in it. The people had been murmuring against God, who had so lately brought them out of Egypt, "and," we read,

"The Lord sent fiery serpents among the people, and they bit the people, and much people of Israel died. Therefore the people came to Moses, and said, We have sinned, for we have spoken against the Lord, and against thee; pray unto the Lord that He take away the serpents from us. And Moses prayed for the people. And the Lord said unto Moses, Make thee a fiery serpent, and set it upon a pole; and it shall come to pass that every one that is bitten, when he looketh upon it, shall live. And Moses made a serpent of brass, and put it upon a pole, and it came to pass, that if a serpent had bitten any man, when he beheld the serpent of brass, he lived" (Numbers 21:6–9).

Very probably the serpent was set up in the centre of the camp, so it would best be seen by all the people; but six hundred thousand men, besides children, and a mixed multitude, must have occupied much camping ground, so that by many of them the brazen serpent must have been seen but as a thin wavy line—a far-away gleam of brass—in the distance. Can you not imagine a man, whose tent was on the verge of the camp, writhing in agony—the fiery venom of the serpent bite scorching the life out of him? and can you not see the one who loved him best, all whose tenderest care could avail him nothing, beseeching him to look at the serpent Moses had set up, pouring into his dull ear all the news she had gathered in the camp of wondrous cures? "Oh, look. Do only look!" And the dying man gasps out in slow, broken speech his unbelief: "What's the good to me of a bit of brass—that little twining thing you talk of, out there? Why, I could hardly make it out." And the loving hands that *would* save, take the poor tortured head that has no power to resist their earnest clasp, and turn the fast glazing eye towards that strange, motionless, uplifted serpent, that seems trembling with life, through her tears. "You *can* see it?" "Yes, I'm looking"; and the fierce fire dies out of the shrivelling veins, and the just sealed eye opens upon new full life, and his ear catches a bursting cry of gratitude and love. Only a look—a dying look!—"*Even so!*"

Your soul can scarcely have come nearer to death than that. A long way off, you can hardly see Christ; but while you feel the agony, you can *look towards* His cross. "When he *beheld* the serpent of brass, he lived." That's *hardly looking*—and our word of utter hope is this, "Behold the Lamb of God, which taketh away the sin of the world" (John 1:29).

When a man feels *no uneasiness* of soul—our *one gleam of hope* for such a one is in that declaration of Scripture—"With God *all things* are possible." He may *yet* feel himself a lost sinner—he may yet look—till then, an uplifted Christ is nothing to him. The man brought off his bitter night-guard into an ambulance, with a frozen limb, does not probably suffer: he tells you smilingly, while sorrowing glances are bent upon him, and the surgeons look gravely at each other, "No pain." Far better for him were his the scorched and mangled form of his comrade on the adjoining pallet, who, brave fellow though he is, cannot repress a shriek of agony as *his* limb is ever so tenderly raised to be dressed. No pain! only—the limb will drop off, unless haply a prompt operation save his life. In the felt despair surely lies the hope. "As Moses lifted up the serpent in the wilderness, *even so* must the Son of man be lifted up; that whosoever believeth in Him should not perish, but have eternal life. For God *so* loved the world, that He gave His only begotten Son, that *whosoever* believeth in Him should not perish, but have everlasting life."

We judge of love, perhaps most of all, by what it bears. Let us read together a few verses that tell us of the last hours in this poor world of ours, of the Son of God who came to die for our sins:—

"He took with Him Peter and the two sons of Zebedee, and began to be sorrowful and very heavy. Then saith He unto them, My soul is exceeding sorrowful, even unto death: tarry ye here, and watch with Me. And He went a little farther, and fell on His face, and prayed, saying, O my Father, if it be possible, let this cup pass from me: nevertheless not as I will, but as Thou wilt.

"And being in an agony He prayed more earnestly: and His sweat was as it were great drops of blood falling down to the ground.

"And when He rose up from prayer, and was come to His disciples, He found them sleeping for sorrow, and said unto them, Why sleep ye? Rise and pray, lest ye enter into temptation.

"And while He yet spake, behold a multitude, and he that was called Judas, one of the twelve, went before them, and drew near unto Jesus to kiss Him. But Jesus said unto him, Judas, betrayest thou the Son of Man with a kiss? When they which were about Him saw what would follow, they said unto Him, Lord, shall we smite with the sword? And one of them smote the servant of the high priest, and cut off his right ear. And Jesus answered and said, Suffer ye thus far. And He touched his ear, and healed him. Then said Jesus, Put up again thy sword into his place—Thinkest thou that I cannot now pray to my Father, and He shall presently give me more than twelve legions of angels? But how then shall the Scriptures be fulfilled, that thus it must be?

"And they all forsook Him, and fled. And they that had laid hold on Jesus led Him away.

"Then did they spit in His face, and buffeted Him; and others smote Him with the palms of their hands, saying, Prophesy unto us, thou Christ, who is he that smote Thee?—Pilate therefore took Jesus, and scourged Him.

"Then the soldiers of the governor took Jesus into the common hall, and gathered unto Him the whole band of soldiers. And they stripped Him, and put on Him a scarlet robe. And when they had platted a crown of thorns, they put it upon His head, and a reed in His right hand: and they bowed the knee before Him, and mocked Him, saying, Hail, King of the Jews! And they spit upon Him, and took the reed, and smote Him on the head. And after that they had mocked Him, they took the robe off from Him, and put His own raiment on Him, and led Him away to be crucified.

"And He bearing His cross went forth into a place called the place of a skull, which is called in the Hebrew Golgotha: where they crucified Him.—And with Him they crucify two thieves; the one on His right hand, and the other on His left.—And sitting down they watched Him there. Then said Jesus, Father, forgive them: for they know not what they do.

"And they that passed by reviled Him, wagging their heads, and saying, Thou that destroyest the temple, and buildest it in three days, save Thyself. If Thou be the Son of God, come down from the cross. Likewise also the chief priests mocking Him with the scribes and elders, said, He saved others; Himself He cannot save.—He trusted in God; let Him deliver Him now, if He will have Him: for He said, I am the Son of God.—The soldiers also mocked Him, coming to Him, and offering Him vinegar, and saying, If thou be the king of the Jews, save thyself.

"And one of the malefactors which were hanged railed on Him, saying, If thou be Christ, save thyself and us. But the other answering rebuked him, saying, Dost thou not fear God, seeing thou art in the same condemnation? And we indeed justly; for we receive the due reward of our deeds: but this man hath done nothing amiss. And he said unto Jesus, Lord, remember me when Thou comest into Thy kingdom. And Jesus said unto him, Verily I say unto thee, to-day shalt thou be with Me in paradise.

"And it was about the sixth hour, and there was a darkness over all the earth until the ninth hour. And the sun was darkened.—And about the ninth hour Jesus cried with a loud voice, saying, Eli! Eli! lama sabacthani? that is to say, My God! my God! why hast Thou forsaken me?—And when Jesus had cried with a loud voice, He said, Father, into Thy hands I commend my spirit: and having said thus, He gave up the ghost" (Matthew 26:37–39, 67, 68; 27:27–31; 37–46; Mark 15:33–37; Luke 22:44–51; 23:34–36, 39–46; John 19:17, 18).

Marvellous Love! is it not? I write, and you surely read, its story with a strange, trembling awe. And all for you and me! Jesus Christ with one God-thought, could have smitten that mocking, insulting throng into hell—could have hurled into darkness and nothingness a lost, wrecked world, the rebel earth on which He was "lifted up." And yet, dear friends, *He could not.* His is an "Everlasting love"; and because the heart of God our Saviour could not, even for one bitter moment, leave off loving us, He let it break! "He hath poured out His soul unto death," and we poor sinners "may have everlasting life."

And had there been but one lost soul on earth—*yours* or *mine*—Christ, I fully believe, would have come down from heaven to die for that soul. "How shall we escape, if we neglect so great salvation"—this "great love wherewith He loved us"? (Hebrews 2:3; Ephesians 2:4). Love is salvation in one syllable. This is God's own question. Will you give Him an answer?

How shall *we* escape? Let us never forget that in all we have been reading of, we had something, it may well be a very great deal, to do—that the sufferings and death of our Lord were, in part, *our work.* We read of those unfathomable sufferings of Christ as a very touching and, we doubt not, a true story. Very likely we feel indignant with that cowardly Pilate who condemned the Saviour—those fierce, brutal Roman soldiers who scourged and buffeted and spat upon Him—that wretched mob of Jews who mocked Him—and we shut up our Testaments. "He was wounded for *our* transgressions, He was bruised for *our* iniquities:—The Lord hath laid on Him *the iniquity of us all*" (Isaiah 53:5, 6). What does that mean? What *can* it mean, but just this: that we, *our own selves,* helped to crucify the Lord Jesus Christ? If not, then Christ never died for *us*—no iniquities *of ours* were "laid on Him." And if He did not bear them for us upon the cross, we must bear them on our souls for ever. When Christ died, more than eighteen hundred years ago, it was "for the sins of the whole world" (1 John 2:2). We nineteenth century men and women, *who are yet sinning* in that world, must confess our share in His bitter agony and death, if we claim to share in His "great salvation." We may not indeed care to put in that claim. *Our only share* may be in the crucifying: *that* we cannot get away from—a solemn thought for some who do not see themselves "sinners," needing God's forgiveness:—guilty of murder, anyhow—accomplices in the death of His Son, however outwardly blameless their lives.

Of course we can refuse this wonderful love. We can, if we will, say desperately "Die" to our wretched souls, and perish. We cannot shut heaven's gates against ourselves. They must remain open while the "Fountain" is open, and all the efforts of sin and Satan are powerless to move their hinges a hair's-breadth; but we can walk straight past them, into that gloom where "the light is as darkness." Any one of us can say to some old, loved sin, that we have often told ourselves we *must be mad* to keep, that has degraded and beggared and made rotten a life, and will follow with cruel memories and scorch with fierce cravings, through eternity—"*I will not* let thee go." We can say to Satan, "I have sold myself to thee, and thou shalt have me"; and God may not interfere, He may let the awful bargain stand!

A man may lie resolutely down on the bank of a full river, and perish with thirst; he can die a pauper if he will, while untold thousands, that he will not claim, stand to his account in the bank; he can go down in the foundering ship, or be burnt to a cinder in the blazing house, with the staunch boat he would not enter, barely clearing the sinking wreck, or the nobly-manned fire-escape resting against his chamber window.

What's your verdict? What does your common sense judge of such a one?

You would call him a sorry seaman who, with the uneasy sea and low, angry mutterings out of the creeping blackness to windward, long warning him of a coming storm, would not take in sail till, with a crash, his masts went by the board, as the tempest swooped down upon the lost ship. You would have some stronger, sterner word to speak your thought of the wretched man if, when his vessel lay a wreck in the trough of the sea, rolling helplessly nearer and nearer to the jagged rocks, and the well-aimed rocket from shore had laid a life-line with steady fall across the drifting hull, he should deliberately cast it off! Shall some of us, dear friends, call ourselves *just what we are?* If we have turned a deaf ear and a closed eye to all God's warnings of the wrath to come, if we have spurned from us His salvation, if we go on spurning it,—when the wrath *is* come, and these poor bodies of ours are breaking up, and our souls are sinking, "how shall we escape?" What would we not give in the beat and crash of that awful sea, might we but clutch the life-line we flung from us, that is floating on the black waters for other wrecked souls to take, for ever out of *our* reach? God knew all about the tempest long before its gloom came upon our horizon, and that's why, while His strong, wise, loving mercy made all ready for the rescue, He would startle our stupid souls with His question, "What will ye do *in the end thereof?*"

A grand thing is the life-line and the strong rope made fast, by which, hand over hand it may be, across the drowning waters, the shore is gained. But why should it come to a wreck? Why out on the angry waters at all? *Get now* a hard grip of His hand that casts the safety-line, who, alike in the wilderness and on the waters, is ever seeking those that are lost. That hand will never let yours go, and "none is able to pluck out of" it. You may not, indeed, always feel the grasp. Satan, who knows that he can never *pluck your hand out of Christ's,* will very often *numb it.* You are none the less safe for that. The clasp is as tight as ever. In all the dark places, and over all the bad places, and through the deep river that none can ford alone, whose waters "take hold" of those who have no hand in theirs, He will lead you safe and wondering, right up into the light and love of His Father's home. "Thy right hand hath holden me up" will explain it all (John 10:28; Psalm 18:35).

CHAPTER X.

THE SURE HOPE.

A WORD about this *feeling*—the *assurance,* about which we are so often anxious.

We find very many people unhappy—even hopeless, because they cannot *feel that they are saved*; as though *their feelings* were necessary to *God's facts*. We don't make ourselves uneasy about the state of our health, much less about our being alive, because we do not feel our hearts beating. Do we? A very blessed thing certainly it is to have assurance, but as certainly it is not necessary to our safety.

In the affairs of this life there are two ways in which we are satisfied as to our having things—by seeing them actually in our own possession, or by taking the word of another that they are ours. Then just take God at His word about salvation. If we have come to God, and asked Him in His own way for salvation, *it is ours*—we are *saved*. "Believe in the Lord Jesus Christ, and thou shalt be saved," says the Bible (Acts 16:3), but nowhere does it say, Thou shalt feel saved. The passenger who, in a dead faint, is lifted into the life-boat, is just as safe as she lies unconscious in the stern-sheets, as the men at the oars. The sleeping child in his cot is just as secure from the beating tempest, as his father who hears its howling, and says, "What a mercy we have a roof over us to-night!"

There are others who cannot believe in their salvation, because they fear they have not felt their sins deeply enough. Their very fear of not having felt sin sufficiently may be, in truth, evidence of its having been felt very deeply. But again, nowhere in the Bible are we told that our sins are blotted out because we have felt their exceeding sinfulness, but simply because we have confessed them. We do not all feel the weight of a burden alike, much may depend on the muscle of the bearer of it, or the steepness of his road; but whoever puts his burden down wants to get rid of it. *Have we got rid of ours?* That is the main thing to be sure of.

If we felt its weight "grievous to be borne" we shall undoubtedly feel the more relief at having laid it down, and the deeper gratitude to Him who took it from us; but the gratitude and the sense of relief come *after the release,* and so can have nothing to do with its being given.

Sure to get home—no fear of that—hand in hand with Christ; but you will have some hard fighting and weary marching, through an enemy's country, mind; and old soldiers will tell you that the night's forced march through the mud and darkness is a deal worse than the morning's action, when the old colours shake out their pierced folds in the early sunlight. Well—as for the fighting—though you very often have to say, Sharp work this! remember, it is always *a battle of three*—God and you against the devil.

The whole Bible is full of strong texts for us to hold on to. We will now take but one, Jesus Christ's own words to some who had not shown themselves very brave, though they all fought a good fight afterwards—"Lo, I am with you alway" (Matthew 28:20). That's for every one under the colours—the one who has just joined and the veteran alike. That text will do, will it not, for the fighting, and the marching too? And there's a wonderful promise—almost the last and the grandest in God's Word—for the end of it all: "He that overcometh" (and we *must* overcome if we have Christ with us, as certainly as we must be miserably beaten if we attempt to march a step or lift an arm in our own strength—the Bible again, "Without Me ye can do *nothing*," (John 15:5)—"He that overcometh shall inherit all things, and I will be his God, and he shall be my son" (Revelation 21:7).

Now, every one of you may say, if he will, "That's for me—I'll have it." A marvellous promise indeed it is, but God has given it, and if it is not too great for Him to give, it is not too great for us to claim.

God's question to us is nowhere, What think ye of yourselves? but, "What think ye of Christ?" It is in the strength of His right hand only that we overcome; in Him alone stands the promise, and it is sure.

The Bible gives us no perhaps; any sort of a hope would not do for us— we want "Thus saith the Lord." Believe *nothing* in the matter of your souls, but what God tells you. Believe *all* He *does tell you*—all about yourself, all about Himself. A man would not put his money into a concern that he had not made the fullest inquiry about; he would not trust himself at sea in a boat, without making sure that her planks were sound—nor in a charge, without seeing that his charger's[1] girths were all right. And shall we trust our souls to an unproved

[1] A "charger" was a horse ridden in battle to charge the enemy. The charger's "girths" were the straps around the horse's body that secured the saddle firmly on the horse. One would not charge into battle against the enemy without making sure the girths to hold the saddle are firmly in place on the horse.

hope? Bring your hope to God's Word; *and if it stands*—if it is a *Bible hope*—then lean on it as hard as you like. Be sure it will bear any strain.

My dear friends, I earnestly trust that, in this poor little book of mine, I have been kept from putting before you anything but the one only Hope that is "an anchor of the soul, both sure and steadfast"; and that I have put *that* plainly forward. The Blood of Jesus Christ, that "cleanseth us from all sin"—"the righteousness of God which is by faith of Jesus Christ unto all and upon all them that believe"—the "faithful saying, worthy of all acceptation, that Christ Jesus came into the world to save sinners" (Hebrews 6:19; 1 John 1:7; Romans 3:22; 1 Timothy 1:15). Out of *these* is forged that anchor that will hold in the heaviest sea, where none of the devil's boats can live, the most deeply sin-laden soul. I have known many throw upon it their whole weight, and never has it failed their trust. How should it? Its holding ground is in "the Rock of Ages"—"Jesus Christ, the same yesterday, and to-day, and for ever" (Hebrews 13:8).

I recollect the last hours of an old sailor, for more than half of his many years a simple, *hard-leaning* Christian. I was bending over him, and said, "Well, old friend, is He with you in the dark valley?" I think it was rather a foolish question of mine, for "the valley of the shadow of death" is just like all other valleys—only dark when there's no light shining in it; and how *could* it be dark if "the Light of the world" was there? Well, my old friend answered me and my mistake with these words, "Dark! why, it's as bright as the noonday sun." *Something real* there—was there not?

Very near and precious too was Jesus Christ to another, whose earthly life counted scarcely nineteen summers—her *true life,* the life "hid with Christ in God" (Colossians 3:3), not nearly so many months. A very child in heart, she went home one glad Christmas morning, as the mists were lifting from the grand old mountains—with long Welsh names as rugged as themselves—whose changing tints and marching shadows it had been her delight, through a long and weary illness, to watch beneath the clustering roses and tangled ivy that might not be trimmed away from her chamber window; from the sun's first peering look over their broken ridges that no one else was awake to greet, till the last dull crimson gleam faded from their steeps. "What a lovely Feast-day!" she said to the sister who first came into her room. Very lovely it was for her. Before the bell of the old white church upon the mountain sounded faintly across the sunlit sands, she was keeping her Christmas in the Father's home above.

In that sweet old story of the Prodigal Son, that we have spoken of, she learnt all the tenderness of God's great love—and how she loved the story ever after! As she read it, she received Jesus in her heart for her own loving Saviour, and was "born again," a daughter of God, by the power of His Spirit (John 1:12). From that hour, "Iesu Grist"[1] was "everything" to her.

During her young life, the wild flowers and hidden ferns, the mossy oaks and rocks, and gleaming sands had been a deep joy to her. She loved them all, and the birds that had their nests in the old grey wood by the shore, and the tiny insects in the flower-cups. She loved all God's dumb creatures; and by their wondrous instinct they knew it. A little shy mouse would come out of its dark home in her sick-room, when no one else was near, and wait unfearing by the side of her bed for the breakfast crumbs, and seem to listen to her loving, child-like talk. Not long before her death she said, "I have been thinking of the dear trees—growing through the night while men are sleeping sweetly. I thought, Perhaps I shall get better, and *I shall see so much more beauty in the world than I have ever seen before*; and I cried a little, to think that I could see *people's* work, but I had not seen Jesus Christ's work, in the trees, and the old rocks, and the tide, up and down, on the sands." Naturally of a fiery temper, an angry word she had spoken made the dear child very sad. "Ah," she said, "I thought the little flowers are always happy. Oh! they *are* happy; blue, and yellow, and pink, all growing up together! *They* never get wild, and *I* got so wild—but I told Jesus Christ of it."

She so loved Sunday. One summer Sunday afternoon, the friend whose happiness it was to find out and meet her every wish said, "I hope to go into the Port to-morrow early, Mary dear, to see about those things you want," and was going on to consult her taste about a little jacket of some light material, for sitting up in bed, that she was very desirous of having, when, with a pained look, she said quickly, "Oh, *please,* dear friend, don't talk about 'Port' to-day, it will grieve Jesus Christ perhaps; you know He gave us six whole days, and only kept one little day for Himself."

Soon after her father was by her bedside. Her favourite chapters had been read to her, but she said suddenly, "Please read to me." "Why, dear, I have just been reading." "Yes, I know, but I want you to read to me," she persisted pleadingly, with a curious little smile on the wasted face. The dear chapter, the fifteenth of Luke, was read; and when she and her own friend were again alone together, the secret came out with almost a little laugh of triumph—"Father was keeping standing by me, and *he would hear my chapter.*"

And when the friend who loved her very dearly, and who has never seen her again, had to leave her, to return home, a very few weeks before she died, although the parting was heavy, and her heart was full, "Little Mary" forgot

---

[1] "Iesu Grist" – Welsh for Jesus Christ. (Prout was a pastor in Nant-y-glo, Wales.)

herself—she always did forget herself—the clasp of the thin, white hand was tight, but she spoke bravely: "I'm so glad my friend's going home; Jesus Christ gave him to me when I was so very bad. I hope to-morrow evening he will be happy with his sisters, perhaps *they* want him now. Perhaps I'll never see you again, but I shall *ask* Jesus Christ to give you back, to say 'Rock of Ages' to me,"—"Graig yr Oesoedd"—that was her loved hymn, learnt by heart in her own language, that it might be said to her the last thing every night, even when the weary eyes could not bear a light to read by. It was sung brokenly by more than a hundred tearful voices over her grave, and the hymn is on its head-stone. "And," she went on to say, "Jesus Christ will come—oh! so quietly—and stop the night with me, and make me remember a verse of 'Prodigal Son' to calm me:—*He's everything to me.*" That reads *real*, my friends, doesn't it? Yes, He was "everything" to His child. In that early Christmas morning, nearly in the words of a beautiful Welsh hymn she liked to hear—

> "One was waiting in the waters—
> 'Jesus Christ'—she knew Him then:
> And the golden gates were open
> Through the mist that filled the glen."

CHAPTER XI.

NEW LIFE AND COMPRESSED LIFE.

You who will read my little book may be of all ages. For all alike this text is waiting: "Behold, *now* is the accepted time; behold, *now* is the day of salvation" (2 Corinthians 6:2). God's "Now" for us—so I believe—is as long as our lives; but how long are they? And as to the youngest I would say, Not too young to die—so to the oldest, Not too old to live. The eleventh hour may have well-nigh ticked out, but a few minutes of the life-day left—it does not take *one* to lift your heart to the Saviour.

All those hours lost? Yes. Bygones must be bygones—God will let them be so. Very precious are the left minutes. Suppose there had been given you a bag full of diamonds, worth some thousands, some hundreds, some tens of pounds; and that, in your ignorance of their value, you had given them nearly all away. If, when but a poor few of your gems remained in the bag, some one told you how precious they were, and that, although you had lost many thousand times the value of what you yet had left, *they* were enough to secure you all you could need for the rest of your days—would you say, "Oh, let them go; they're not worth the keeping"—would you just fling them after the others? I don't think you would.

To some of you may be given yet many years—to some but few. At its longest, "the time is short" (1 Corinthians 7:29). A little or a big bit of life joined on to eternity counts only for the work done in it, that determines which eternity it is a part of. "Happy New Year" is a hearty, cheery greeting that one likes to give and to get: but it's poor wishing, after all, if we do not wish our friends something better than any number of happy new years, since *the last* will have to be put upon our coffin-lid and grave-stone. Before the close of the year, you and I may wish one another "Happy Eternity to you!" This, dear friends, we have very plainly seen, is *God's wish* for every one of us.

I wish you many happy years too, all "new" ones, if they are to be really happy ones. It is part of the same wish. For when a man becomes a Christian, he is born again (John 3:7), and the eternity-life, in a sense, *begins*. "*This* is life eternal, that they might know Thee, the only true God, and Jesus Christ whom Thou hast sent," are the Saviour's own words.

With that wonderful new life comes new work; the new life and the new work begin at the same instant. Here is another surprising text, also Christ's words, very like the other—"*This* is the work of God, that ye believe on Him whom He hath sent." Till this work *in* our own souls is done, not one stroke of true work *for* God can be done by us. It would be strange gardening to say, "No good planting this tree! it bears no fruit." How can it, till it is "rooted and grounded"? (John 17:3; 6:29; Ephesians 3:17). Once *really alive*—it is not so much that you have *got to work,* as that you will not be able to keep from working. It is difficult to believe in such a dismal dead-alive thing as a do-nothing Christian. You may indeed seem to yourself but half alive—but Life is life, just as Sin is sin. Those marvellous moving atoms in duckweed, ten thousand millions of which, we are told to our amazement, would but make up the bulk of a single hemp seed, are as much alive as Elephants. "Who hath despised the day of small things?" (Zechariah 4:10).

That is a grand rule for *all work* that we find in the Bible (Ecclesiastes 9:10)—"Whatsoever thy hand findeth to do, do it with thy might." And a strong reason enforces it—"For there is no work, nor device, nor knowledge, nor wisdom, in the grave whither thou goest."

"*Thy* might"—that's comforting for some of us who are conscious of not being over strong. A child may put out his "might" in uprooting a weed, as truly as the strong man whose muscular arm wrenches from its bed a mass of stone. And here is another word for us all, "My strength is made perfect in weakness." "To them that have *no* might He increaseth strength" (2 Corinthians 12:9; Isaiah 40:29).

So, let none of us be limp, loose-jointed working Christians. Do not any of you, my friends, be "water-porridge men"—as those pithy fellows the Bechuanas say—while you may have abundance of "milk, without money and without price," and "grow thereby."

And do not lead see-saw lives, up to-day and down to-morrow. Let hearty, steady, all-along work be the evidence of deep, warm, earnest life. It's only the surface-water that freezes. Let us make up our minds that the remainder of life to each of us, be it much or little, shall be *compressed life*—something like those compact, workmanlike bales, so tightly and evenly bound with black or yellow iron bands, that I have once and again stopped to admire, as the laden lorries glided slowly along the streets of Manchester, a small fortune in each bale—life, with as much as possible of the best work, of the one, only true pattern, compressed into its years or its months by the "Love that constraineth us" (2 Corinthians 5:14).

Love is our motto-word for all the work, as it is our foundation-word for all the hope. If "we have known and believed the love that God hath to us," we shall, in our poor way, *love Him*, "and this commandment have we from Him, that he that loveth God love his brother also" (1 John 4:16–23). Perhaps it would be hardly too much to say, There's nothing Love cannot do. As a dear old poet who wrote some two centuries and a-half ago, says—

> "Love is swift of foot;
>   Love's a man of war,
>   And can shoot,
>   And can hit from far."

How it is that love is so very strong, we find out from the 7th verse of the chapter just quoted from—"Love is of God." He "*is love*," you remember.

Our main work *for* God, let us remember, is to bring others, young and old, *to* God. As a thoroughly in earnest, original Cornishman put it—"It's soul-catching." If you have taken the firm grip of Christ's hand with one of yours, get hold of somebody else—or rather, keep getting hold of somebody—with the other, and *pull them up on the rock,* alongside of you. Do not let people drown all around you, without trying to grasp and save. Don't fear for your arm; reach down into the cold, dashing waves. The Hand that holds gives strength to the hand that reaches. No saved man belongs to himself. We have Bible again for that—"Ye are not your own; ye are bought with a price: therefore glorify God in your body, and in your spirit, which are God's" (1 Corinthians 6:19, 20).

Let us never forget the words, "Lo, I am with you alway," when we are trying to do a poor bit of work for Him who spoke them. If sometimes we feel all alone, it is not that God has left us, but that we have left Him. We say, "The sun has set." The sun has done nothing of the kind. He has not stirred from his place in the heavens. 'Tis we, who have been spinning away to the East, some five hundred and eighty miles an-hour, putting our eight thousand miles of dull, heavy earth between ourselves and his steady light. "I the Lord change not," declares God of Himself, "with whom is no variableness, neither *shadow* of turning" (Malachi 3:6; James 1:17).

Often, indeed, shall we be terribly perplexed as to what is the thing we really ought to do. As a well-known preacher once said, "Conscience is an excellent chronometer, but it must sometimes be brought to the sun-dial." How am I by the Bible? We need never be long in doubt, the guiding shadow-line falls clear and strong across the dial—but fast or slow, *we must not mind moving the hands.* "If any of you lack wisdom, let him ask of God, that giveth to all men liberally, and upbraideth not; and it shall be given him," is the promise of clear guidance to all who ask for it. "This is the way, walk ye in it," may be read by us, even in our hastiest duty—"He may run that readeth"—by the light of "the Holy Spirit" which God has plainly promised "to them that ask Him," upon a text just glanced at or remembered (James 1:5; Isaiah 30:21; Habakkuk 2:2; Luke 11:13).

Let the way be pitch dark, so that we cannot see an inch of our path before us, here is our word—"Who is among you that feareth the Lord, that obeyeth the voice of His servant, that walketh in darkness, and hath no light? Let him trust in the name of the Lord, and stay upon his God" (Isaiah 50:10). *That* is just *keeping hold of Christ's hand.* We must not, though, miss the conditions. This loving command to "stay upon his God" is given to him only who fears God, and who obeys the voice of Him who, for us men, and for our salvation, "took upon Him the form of a servant" (Philippians 2:7); in other words, for him who has truly come to Christ. The very same condition belongs to that other text just quoted about God's giving to all men liberally; it goes on, "But let him ask in faith."

CHAPTER XII.

REST AND COMFORT.

BUT, however much we may be in earnest, however honestly we may seek guidance, a heavy heart will often make heavy work. " Man is born unto trouble, as the sparks fly upward," said one of old who meant to comfort a friend who had his full share of it (Job 5:7). You may believe *your* burthen of life's cares and sorrows hardly lighter than Job's—yet, under them all, and though the work may drag, you shall work on if you will—with a heart at rest *for the future.* People usually send the title-deeds of their estates to their lawyers, to be kept safely for them in strong, fire-proof safes. " I know whom I have believed," said Paul, " and am persuaded that He is able to keep that which I have committed to Him against that day "—" in the which the heavens shall pass away with a great noise, and the elements shall melt with fervent heat, the earth also, and the works that are therein, shall be burned up" (2 Timothy 1:12; 2 Peter 3:10). The apostle had " committed" *the keeping of his soul to Christ,* and had no fear of its being taken all care of.

" If I were only ready to die!" There are, perhaps, few expressions that those who visit the sick more often hear. The soul committed to Christ's safe keeping—that is the whole secret of being " ready"—ready to die, and at the same time, ready to live; for here, too, is to be found the true reading of a very favourite maxim with many, " Make the best of both worlds." No better rule of life, so long as we are quite sure it *is* " the best." Unfortunately those who use this saying the oftenest make a miserably poor affair of this world, and the very worst of the other.

A story is told of Whitefield, how, calling upon a Christian lady of his acquaintance, who had just been " burnt out," in her comfortless lodgings, he came up with a cheery smile, and, heartily shaking her hand, said, " Madam, I wish you joy." She was silent with amazement, thinking her friend and pastor, if not gone crazy, was strangely unfeeling. And Whitefield answered her silence—"I give you joy, madam, that you have your best treasure where no fire can touch it."

But we must not suppose that our Father in heaven, who puts His children's most precious things so carefully away for them in His own home, has no thought of their griefs and difficulties and worries down here. What does this mean—"Casting all your care upon Him, for He careth for you"? (1 Peter 5:7). As it has been said, there is no loop-hole of sin but there is some word in the Bible that exactly fits it, and fills it up, so there is no aching want that there is not some soothing word to fill. When a crushing grief has fallen upon some home, and "the whole stay of bread" is taken away with a precious life, God says to the desolate hearts, "I, even I, am He that comforteth you—As one whom his mother comforteth, so will I comfort you—thy Maker is thy husband."

I do like the saying of an earnest loving-hearted old body who was comforting a sorrowing child: "You see, I was just feeling her feelings for her, dear lamb!" Christ, dear friends, *feels all our feelings.* He is "touched with the feeling of our infirmities." In the deepest depths of sorrow, "His own" often know most of the light of His presence,—fathoms down in the blackness of the mine-shaft, men who look straight up into the midday sky see the stars.

And when, in the soul-sadness which is heaviest of all, "they that are Christ's" write bitter things against themselves—when overborne, utterly broken, in the well-nigh hopeless fight with sin, they hear, and almost believe, the cruel whisper that they are "none of His"—into the desolation and despair comes a loving voice: "Fear not: for I have redeemed thee, I have called thee by thy name; thou art Mine" (Isaiah 51:12; 66:13; 54:5; 43:1; Hebrews 4:15).

Shall we turn for some teaching here to a child's words? I don't like to leave their story untold, for it is one of the deepest and sweetest of those lessons that we may so often learn through the little ones. It is indeed only for those who have "come" in God's own way, who have "received" Christ into their hearts as their Saviour, alike from the punishment and the power of their sin, and are the sons and daughters of God; but to them it will be very precious. A little girl of three years old, who had thus early been taught by Christian parents to love Jesus, and to believe herself one of His "lambs," had one day been naughty, as all children will be sometimes; and some not very wise relative said to her, "I thought you were one of Christ's lambs; *you're* not a lamb, I'm sure." The dear little thing was almost broken-hearted. Why, she was *sure* she was a lamb. For a long time she was silent and very sorrowful, and could not be consoled. Suddenly the sweet, tearful face got back all its old sunny look, and, with wonderful glee, she almost sang out the precious secret that had come to her—"Yes, auntie, me *am* Christ's 'ittle lamb—me am *Christ's naughty lamb.*" Let us all take, with deep, humble thankfulness, the lesson, as that dear child brings it to our hearts, and ask God, with the adoption and the confidence of children, to give us more and more of their simple, trusting love.

CHAPTER XIII.

THE AIM AND THE CLAIM.

I FEAR, dear friends, I may have said a tiresome deal too much, even while I seem to want to say much more. But as I write, the awful, the stupendous reality of those things I have ventured to speak about, makes me feel how miserably small and powerless is all that I have said, and may well weight my heart with the thought that they may have been "things too wonderful for me, which I knew not." I daresay, too, that I have said things over and over again; but the melody of the Gospel message, sweet and full as it is, in truth, is on so few notes, that they are ever coming back. The Gospel is for "every creature" (Mark 16:6), because, as we have seen, sin is every creature's disease—eternity every creature's certainty; and so, very simple, for every creature's ear, is the strain in which the "old, old story" of Redeeming Love has been told, all down the centuries, since the garden gates of Eden were closed, to this day. Weak words, dear friends, all these of mine—but I have clinched them with strong texts, that many of you, I hope, will find out, and prove for yourselves.

And now, I must really begin to end. There is a thought I would like to leave with you: I am not sure that it is my own, it turned up in an old note-book, in which I had jotted things down from time to time, in a not very orderly fashion, and it is something like this. God's plan of salvation may be likened to the rings of a target. There is the outer black ring of Sin, and close within, the red ring of The Blood, and within that, the white ring of Righteousness, circling the golden centre of Glory; each ring clearly marked right round, no running of the colours one into the other, no getting into the white, save through the red circle, nor into the centre, but by the white. *Make sure,* my friends, if you will bear this target in mind, that you get out of the big black circle of your sin—whether you are on its inner or its outer rim makes "no difference" (Romans 3:23)—and *aim straight at the Gold.*

Well—this, after all, is only man's thought about himself and about salvation, and I would much rather end with one of God's own thoughts about Himself and us. A wonderful thought it is, and in very wonderful words has God spoken it. In them, if in any words in His Bible, He says to us poor sinners, "Never, *never* say 'Die' to your souls."

These words were a stronghold and a quiet resting-place to one weary, shuddering soul, pursued by the cruel memory of her sin, who had been utterly unable to get peace from other precious assurances of God's unwearying, changeless love. I cannot tell how it was I turned to them: in truth, the words, now the marked ones in my Bible that I can best *hold on to,* had never before attracted my close attention. God, I suppose, turned the page for His dying, hopeless child. The words are these—"Thou hast made Me to serve with thy sins, thou hast wearied Me with thine iniquities. I, even I, am He that blotteth out thy transgressions for Mine own sake, and will not remember thy sins. Put Me in remembrance" (Isaiah 43:24–26). They *are* marvellous words, are they not? As I read them by that dying girl, rather than to her—for it seemed as though God *had* "forgotten to be gracious," and had no word for her—there came a dawn of hope into the poor wistful eyes that were looking out into the darkness.

"You don't mean to say those words are there? Read them again—now, again. They'll do."

I cannot now remember any after-words. Yes, "they'll do" *for us all,* dear friends of mine: for him who writes, whose sins have so long wearied and made to serve his loving, waiting God, and for you who will read them here.

Do just think of their condescension, and their infinite fulness of strong love. "Put Me in remembrance," says Jehovah—remind Me of what I have said—hold Me to My word! Say to the God whom you have made your servant by your sin, Forgive it all—blot it all out—forget it—*you said you would!* God *will let* us poor lost ones say this to Him. My brother, my sister—as you lay down this poor little book, do put God in remembrance. Tell Him that He has promised to cast out none that come to Him, and that *you* are come; that *you claim,* for *Jesus Christ's sake,* forgiveness, and holiness, and peace, and everlasting life. That's great asking; but in the "name which is above every name" you ask; and it does not get beyond His own "whatsoever," and His "all things"; even as His "whosoever" and His "every one" take in each and all of us. Thank God for the alls and the whosoevers—yes, on both sides,—where should we be without them? "God hath concluded them all in unbelief—that He might have mercy on all" (Philippians 2:19; John 14:13; Matthew 21:22; John 3:15, 16; Luke 11:10; Romans 11:32).

What shall be my last words? They must not be my own. I would like them, too, to bring back the thought with which we began. We will take the "I know" of God our Saviour, given to us in the last verse of the twelfth of John—that makes sure knowing *for us*. "THE FATHER WHICH SENT ME, HE GAVE ME A COMMANDMENT, WHAT I SHOULD SAY, AND WHAT I SHOULD SPEAK. AND I KNOW THAT HIS COMMANDMENT IS LIFE EVERLASTING."

"See that ye refuse not HIM that speaketh" (Hebrews 12:25).

Loving—All Along!

TRAMP—tramp, on the downward way,
With seldom a stop, and never a stay:
Loving the darkness—hating the light;
Our faces set towards Eternal night—
      Each has answered God's cry,
   "Why will ye die?
        Turn ye—turn ye." "Not I—not I!"
We have bartered away His gems and gold
For the foulest things that earth's gutters hold.
We have told Him to spare, or strike, as He will—
Do His best to save, or His worst to kill—
Have laughed at the devil's tightening chains,
   And bidden him forge them strong—
     And God has kept on loving us!
      Loving—all along!

The Love still follows, as we tramp on—
A sorrowful fall in its pleading tone:
"With mercies great will I gather thee;
I have called thee by name—Return to Me.
Thou wilt tire in the dreary ways of sin;
I left My home—to bring *thee* in.
      In its golden street
    Stand no weary feet;—
       Its rest is glorious—its songs are sweet."
And we shout back angrily, hurrying on
To a terrible home, where rest is none:
"We want not your city's gilded street,
   Nor to hear its constant song"—
     And still God keeps on loving us!
      Loving—all along!

And the tender Voice pursues each one:
"Dear sinner, what more could thy God have done?
Thou hast made Me to serve with thy bitter strife—
Thy sin has wearied, in Heaven, My life.

My Heaven! yet its light I could not see,
When, alone in the darkness, I died for thee.
      Thy sin of this day,
    In its shadow, lay
        Between My face and One turned away!"
And we stop, and turn for a moment's space,
To fling back His love in the Saviour's face,—
To give His heart yet another grief,
    And glory in the wrong—
      And Christ is always loving us!
        Loving—all along!

One is bending low before the King;
And the Angels listen—with quivering wing:
A wondering awe on each glad, grand face,
At the joy of their Lord on His Throne of Grace.
He has entered the city, and sings its hymn;
While the gold of its street through tears is dim:
"To Him who so loved me and washed me white,
To Him be all honour, and power, and might!"
      That marvellous Love
    No sin could move,
        Waited and wearied not—sought and strove—
Followed unchanging, the whole dark way,
        And led into full, Eternal Day.

Just like our own, mad, hastening feet!
They stopped—to listen. They turned—to meet.
The gates of pearl are standing wide,
And the souls press in on every side.
To *us*, through the darkness, the voice still calls
From the gleaming heights of those jasper walls.
Wilderness weary—mired with sin,
We, with the rest, may enter in:
Each welcomed home to the place long kept
    Among the exulting throng—
      And God will still be loving us!
        Loving us—all along!

Never Say Die ended with the poem by Prout, "Loving All Along." Frances set this to music, and the score is given next.

LOVING ALL ALONG.

Words by Samuel Gillespie Prout.

Music by Frances R. Havergal.

1. Tramp, tramp on the down-ward way, With sel-dom a stop and ne-ver a stay, Lov ing the dark-ness, ha-ting light, Our fa - ces set to wards e-ter - nal

night! Each has ans-wered God's cry, "Why will ye die?

Turn ye! turn ye!" "Not I, not I!" We have

bar-tered a-way His— gems and gold For the emp-ty husks and the

sha - dows cold; We have laugh'd at the De - mon's tight - 'ning chains, And

bid-den him forge them strong! And   God has kept on   lov - ing us,

Chorus   Andante ad. lib.

Lov ing, all ___ a - long! And God has kept on lov - ing us, Lov - ing, all a-

bring thee in! In its   gold - en___ street Stand___ no wea - ry
died for thee! Thy___   sin of this day,   In its sha - dow___

feet,   Its rest is   glor - ious, its songs are___ sweet!"
lay   Be - tween My   face___ and One turn'd a - way!"

Allegro

And we   shout back an - gri-ly,   hurry - ing   on   To a
And we   stop and   turn for a   mo - ment's space,   Fling - ing

Lov - ing, all   a - long!
Lov - ing, all   a - long!

4.One is   bend ing low be-

fore   the   King, And   the An - gels lis - ten with   quiv - 'ring   wing,   He has

en - tered the Ci - ty and   sings   its   hymn, While the gold of its streets   thro'

sought and strove! To_ us through the dark ness, the Voice still calls From the

gleam-ing heights of the jas-per walls; To the long kept pla-ces our wel come waits, A-

mid the exul ting throng. And God will still be lov - ing us, Lov ing all_ a-

Chorus
ad. lib.

Will You Not Come?

"Thou hast received gifts for men; yea, for the rebellious also."—Psalm 68:18.

John 5:40
Ezekiel 33:11
John 10:11
Romans 6:23
2 Cor. 5:20

WILL you not come to Him for life?
Why will ye die, oh why?
He gave His life for you, for you!
The gift is free, the word is true!
Will you not come? oh, why will you die?

Acts 10:36
Colossians 1:20
1 Peter 1:19
Romans 5:15, 18
Ephesians 2:14

Will you not come to Him for peace—
Peace through His cross alone?
He shed His precious blood for you;
The gift is free, the word is true!
He is our Peace! oh, is He your own?

Jeremiah 6:16
Matthew 11:28
Isaiah 11:10
Isaiah 28:12
Hebrews 4:3, 9

Will you not come to Him for rest?
All that are weary, come!
The rest He gives is deep and true;
'Tis offered now, 'tis offered you!
Rest in His love, and rest in His home.

Matthew 13:44
John 16:24
Philippians 2:7, 8
John 15:11
Romans 15:13

Will you not come to Him for joy,—
Will you not come for this?
He laid His joys aside for you,
To give you joy, so sweet, so true!
Sorrowing heart, oh, drink of the bliss!

Ephesians 3:19
Psalm 107:9
Ephesians 2:4
Revelation 1:5
Romans 5:8

Will you not come to Him for love—
Love that can fill the heart,
Exceeding great, exceeding free?
He loveth you, He loveth me!
Will you not come? Why stand you apart?

John 4:14
Psalm 34:8
Isaiah 30:18
Matthew 7:7, 8
John 7:37

Will you not come to Him for *all?*
Will you not "taste and see"?
He waits to give it all to you;
The gifts are free, the words are true!
Jesus is calling, "Come unto Me!"

Frances Ridley Havergal

Made in the USA
Middletown, DE
08 March 2017